# THE ULTIMATE

# IN

# RIFLE ACCURACY

A handbook for those who seek the ultimate in rifle accuracy;
whether it be for competition, testing, or hunting.

GLENN NEWICK

**Stoeger Publishing**®
*Great Outdoor Books & More Since 1924*

## STOEGER PUBLISHING COMPANY IS A DIVISION OF BENELLI U.S.A.

### BENELLI U.S.A.
*Vice President and General Manager:*
Stephen Otway
*Vice President of Marketing and Communications:*
Stephen McKelvain

### STOEGER PUBLISHING COMPANY
*President:* Jeffrey Reh
*Publisher:* Jay Langston
*Managing Editor:* Harris J. Andrews
*Design & Production Director:*
Cynthia T. Richardson
*Photography Director:* Alex Bowers
*Imaging Specialist:* William Graves
*National Sales Manager:* Jennifer Thomas
*Special Accounts Manager:* Julie Brownlee
*Publishing Associate:* Christine Lawton
*Administrative Assistant:* Shannon McWilliams

*Cover Design & Photography:* Ray Wells

Published 2004 by
Stoeger Publishing Company
17603 Indian Head Highway, Suite 200
Accokeek, Maryland 20607

BK6465
ISBN: 0-88317-159-7

Manufactured in the United States of America.

Distributed to the book trade and
to the sporting goods trade by:
Stoeger Industries
17603 Indian Head Highway, Suite 200
Accokeek, Maryland 20607
301-283-6300 Fax: 301-283-6986
www.stoegerbooks.com

**OTHER PUBLICATIONS:**
Shooter's Bible
  The World's Standard Firearms
  Reference Book
Gun Trader's Guide
  Complete Fully Illustrated
  Guide to Modern Firearms with
  Current Market Values

**HUNTING & SHOOTING**
The Turkey Hunter's Tool Kit:
  Shooting Savvy
Archer's Bible
Trailing the Hunter's Moon
Shotgunning for Deer
Hunting Whitetails East & West
Hunt Club Management Guide
Complete Book of
  Whitetail Hunting
Hunting and Shooting
  with the Modern Bow
Elk Hunter's Bible
The Ultimate in Rifle Accuracy
Advanced Black Powder Hunting
Hunting America's Wild Turkey
Taxidermy Guide
Cowboy Action Shooting
Great Shooters of the World
Hounds of the World
Labrador Retrievers

**COLLECTING BOOKS**
Sporting Collectibles
The Working Folding Knife
The Lore of Spices

**FIREARMS**
Antique Guns
P-38 Automatic Pistol
The Walther Handgun Story
Complete Guide to
  Compact Handguns
Complete Guide to Service
  Handguns
America's Great Gunmakers
Firearms Disassembly
  with Exploded Views
Rifle Guide
Gunsmithing at Home
The Book of the Twenty-Two
Complete Guide to Modern Rifles
Complete Guide to Classic Rifles
Legendary Sporting Rifles

FN Browning Armorer
  to the World
Modern Beretta Firearms
How to Buy & Sell Used Guns
Heckler & Koch:
  Armorers of the Free World
Spanish Handguns

**RELOADING**
The Handloader's Manual of
  Cartridge Conversions
Modern Sporting Rifle Cartridges
Complete Reloading Guide

**FISHING**
Bassing Bible
Ultimate Bass Boats
The Flytier's Companion
Deceiving Trout
The Complete Book
  of Trout Fishing
The Complete Book of Flyfishing
Peter Dean's Guide to Fly-Tying
The Flytier's Manual
Flytier's Master Class
Handbook of Fly Tying
The Fly Fisherman's
  Entomological Pattern Book
Fiberglass Rod Making
To Rise a Trout
Flyfishing for Trout - A to Z
Fishing Online:
  1,000 Best Web Sites
Fishing Made Easy

**MOTORCYCLES & TRUCKS**
The Legend of Harley-Davidson
The Legend of the Indian
Best of Harley-Davidson
Classic Bikes
Great Trucks
4X4 Vehicles

**COOKING GAME**
Fish & Shellfish Care & Cookery
Game Cookbook
Dress 'Em Out
Wild About Venison
Wild About Game Birds
Wild About Freshwater Fish
Wild About Seafood
World's Best Catfish Cookbook

# Forward

Some say the sport of benchrest shooting along with its gadgetry, precision and techniques is one of the best kept secrets in the shooting world. The relative scarcity of books on the subject would tend to bear this out. Efforts by key individuals in organized benchrest competition have often been directed toward swelling our numbers but have never made this sport as large as some of the other shooting disciplines.

The author of this work has attempted to offer some historical background as part of this treatise. More than this, he has attempted to put in perspective where the sport has been, where it is now, and some hints on where it is going. Persons, places, equipment, techniques and practices are discussed in terms of this unique contribution to the development of that mysterious sport called benchrest shooting.

It has been since 1973, when Warren Page published THE ACCURATE RIFLE, that this sport was treated in an authoritative fashion regarding its tools and procedures. The author here is bringing the "rest shooter" up to date, so to speak, with equipment and practices put into use during the past sixteen years. For those who practice stool shootin competitively, there is much food for thought here and perhaps some techniques and explanations not yet considered by even yourselves. For the beginner or one contemplating a try of this challenging sport, a veritable wealth of information is contained between the covers. It would be tremendously difficult to get all of your questions answered from a single source. This book attempts to do this and goes so far as even walking you through an imaginary match, explaining many of the things old timers take for granted, but beginners are generally too timid to ask about.

The author has the proper credentials to attempt a work such as this. He began his competitive benchrest shooting in the early years of this decade. You will read about some of his failures as well as some of his successes. As a relative beginner, he won the coveted 3-Gun Aggregate title for International Benchrest Shooters, itself an unheard of accomplishment. Additionally, he has set several international records, some of which still stand today. Glenn is somewhat unique regarding the age at which he began shooting registered benchrest. Most pursuers of the "one hole" group don't begin their formal competition until they have a fair number of years and many practice rounds fired behind them. He, on the other hand, began in his early 20's and got right into competition. I believe his success bears out the theory that young eyes, quick responses and the drive of youth to excel can pay handsome dividends.

Having shot scores of matches with Glenn beginning with his first and right up to the present, I can attest to the accuracy of his work here. He has explained in these pages what he feels were his strengths and weaknesses while developing as a competitive shooter. Like most of the rest of this fine segment of the shooting sports, Glenn has developed a wit and awareness that has made him a pleasant shooter to share a loading bench with. It is not only the precision, the challenge, or the elements that make the sport of benchrest shooting a great one, but mostly the people in it. In reading this book I believe you may begin to feel a sort of kinship with some of the personalities mentioned. You may even empathize with their problems or situations encountered. If this should take place or for whatever reason may strike you, I hope you, the reader, will gain the interest and accept the challenge much as the author initially did and become part of the people and practices that make the sport of benchrest shooting all that it is today.

Finally, the sport owes Glenn Newick a round of applause for preparing such a treatise. It was long overdue and has been handled in a thorough and competent manner. We are enriched by his efforts.

Robert A. (Bob) White
Three term president of International
Benchrest Shooters Association.

# TABLE OF CONTENTS

# Preface

There's a famous saying that every person in the world has at least one book in them. This is mine. With no books on Benchrest since Warren Page's excellent THE ACCURATE RIFLE it's certainly time to give a current source to the general shooting public. Often, it's the written word that spurs people to try new sports. This book will be informative for those who already participate in Benchrest, either in competition, or for fun. Where it will be most valuable is to the shooter on the fringe, who pounds away with a 7 Mag, or a .243, who travels to the range every Sunday to try for that elusive small group. Benchrest rifles are capable of a 100 yard group below two tenths of an inch every time they're shot in good conditions. I want those who struggle for a half inch group to know the thrill of getting upset when a four shot group of .150″ is spoiled all the way out to .315″. For less than the cost of a new fibreglass hunting rifle, and scope, a shooter can buy a used benchrest rifle, scope, dies, brass and bullets. The only fun rifles are accurate ones, why not step up to the most accurate rifles in the world.

There are others in benchrest who are more intelligent, there are several who write better stories, there are a few who shoot smaller groups. There have been many, who too found the right conditions on a calm overcast day, at a place like the Council Cup range, and shot an aggregate under the existing record. And made me second. – or third. It's that friendly competition which makes this sport so valuable.

If you have any interest at all in shooting accurate rifles get a membership in either IBS or NBRSA. Add to the NBRSA membership a subscription to PRECISION SHOOTING Magazine and you'll be fully informed on the current happenings of the benchrest world.

This book is for the betterment of Benchrest. Jack Sutton, who does a lot of the work on HART rifle barrels, helped jump start this project by commenting on one of the articles I wrote for PRECISION SHOOTING Magazine. He said the article explained the topic in a clear, straight forward manner. That's the second goal for this book. Once we get past the safety chapter there won't be a lot of preaching. Different sides of the story will be presented fairly, go ahead and look at all the advice, then make your own conclusions on the information. Besides - If you're really a benchrest shooter, you make your own decisions anyway.

Yours is the thrill from tiny groups

Good luck

Glenn Newick
Houston, Texas

# 1

# *Safety*

Safety is the first chapter for a reason. Shooting can be the most enjoyable form of entertainment there is, involving the mind and body in a test of skill and ability; however, it has the possibility of changing to a disaster with one careless accident.

Please remember safety in all phases of the shooting sports. Use proper storage containers for powder and primers, keep components and arms under lock and key. Don't give children access to things for which they don't understand the danger. Don't smoke while handling components (there was an accident last year where a benchrest shooter was badly burned by powder accidently ignited while reloading) neck sized benchrest cases rarely fail in use, but still, check for split necks during your loading process. Pistol primers are made with a thinner cup than the one used in small rifle primers. The full house loads shot in benchrest rifles would pierce the cup easily, and release high pressure gas back into the action. Seat primers to the bottom of the primer pocket. Primers showing above the case head cause erratic ignition, with its resultant erratic accuracy, and possible slam-fires in semi-automatic rifles. Cleanliness and organization at the loading table helps prevent distractions and unintentional mistakes. Return components to the proper containers when the loading cycle is completed. For the sake of your eyesight get in the habit of wearing safety glasses while reloading and shooting.

During transportation to the range keep all firearms and ammunition safely secured. Observe the bolts out rule at all times, even if you are the only person at the range. When checking bullet jam use dummy cartridges. Be careful of accidental discharges: a 2 oz. trigger can be delicate. Please make sure the rifle isn't loaded till pointed down range. Don't let a shot escape over the backstop. With the recent introduction of factory PPC rifles and loaded ammunition we must be especially careful. With most custom benchrest rifles set up with a tight neck chamber, A SAKO factory round could cause extreme pressure problems if forced into an undersized neck. Most custom rifles have their neck dimension stamped on the barrel. If you're not sure, have a competent gunsmith check for clearance. Safety is a permanent state of mind, both for yourself, and for those around you.

### Here are the ten commandments of firearms safety:

Treat every gun with the respect due a loaded gun. (Read this one twice, it's the most important of all.)

Be sure of your target before you pull the trigger.

Always be sure the barrel and action are clear of obstructions.

Never point your gun at anything you do not want to shoot.

Never leave your gun unattended unless you unload it first.

Avoid alcoholic beverages both before and during shooting.

Never climb a tree or cross a fence with a loaded gun.

Never shoot at a hard, flat surface or the surface of water. Always make sure you have a safe backstop

Carry only empty guns, taken down or with the action open, into your camp, car, or home.

Store guns and ammunition separately under lock and key.

As much as the constant competitor thinks they know about firearms safety, I've seen most of these commandments violated. Often we go from the loading area to the firing line with the muzzle swinging over the shoulder, and pointing every which way. Misfires and stuck loaded rounds must be handled with extreme caution. Using a cleaning rod to knock out a stuck round has resulted in fatal injury when the cartridge went off. Talk about a moment of thoughtlessness: shoot a rifle with an obstructed barrel. Cleaning rods, used to clear brass stuck in the chamber, have been accidently shot down range. I can show you the picture of a barrel that was shot with the bore sighting spud still in the muzzle. It's a credit to todays manufacturers the equipment is as safe and well built as it is. Most of the lawsuits involving manufacturers are the result of improper gun handling; not from faulty manufacture. Don't become a statistic.

With all the negative publicity improper use of firearms gets please strive for perfect safety performance. Look into your own shooting experience and rectify problems before they cause an accident. Let the shooter next to you know you won't tolerate unsafe behavior. It's up to all of us to keep this, the finest of sports, safe.

# 2

# *History*

The invention of gunpowder goes back long before the earliest firearms. The Chinese and Hindus are thought to have had it in the time of Moses. The crude hand weapons of the 1300's and 1400's were more useful scaring horses and peasants than in efficiently hitting an aimed mark. Development of the matchlock gave the world it's first aimed hand firearm, samples from the early 1500's show crude front and rear sights. It was the heavy ball thrown by these devices which ended the reign of the armored knight. Where before an arrow or bolt would glance off their armour these bullets could kill from afar. It was a good thing the days of the mounted knight finally ended. To resist the flying balls protective armour had grown thick and heavy, so heavy horses could barely convey the knights to the field of battle. The wielder of the matchlock wasn't much better off, his equipment was almost as cumbersome as the knights.

Another important component of an accurate rifle is the rifling itself: that came from Nuremberg in the fifteenth century. The next major improvement was the Wheel-Lock: an example in the Dresden Museum is dated to 1510. This invention removed the problem of keeping a wick alight in damp conditions. When the arm was triggered a spring driven device ignited the priming for the arm. A wondrous article for it's day; however even Lester Bruno couldn't shoot a good group with one!

Switzerland shows a record of shooting from a rest in the 1600's; however no targets remain from that era to show the accuracy levels attained. Development of the flintlock, in the years just before 1630, made the advent of modern accuracy possible. Believed to be of Spanish origin, the flintlock made the Kentucky rifle with an explorer standing behind it conceivable.

The American rifleman has a long and storied history. Use of the rifle for the everyday food pot gave the adventurer and settler his skill as a marksman. Each shot was justified. This accounting for every shot held him in good stead when the country fought for it's independence. The rifleman remembered the lessons the Indian had taught about concealment and individual aimed shots. The British Soldier fought in the European method. Massed ranks and volley fire with smooth bore Brown Bess Muskets weren't effective when the opponent was hiding behind a log.

Those lessons we learned in the wilderness were taught to every boy who grew up in an appropriate area. The changing face of America has removed these lessons from a huge part of the population. The biggest complaint on a basic training firing line is the low level of marksmanship in the recruits. Small wonder that a recent survey in New York City showed only one in ten people even knew someone who hunted.

The modern sport of benchrest shooting was kick started in 1944 with the Puget Sound Snipers Congress, though there have been many instances through history where something very similar has been practiced. In the book OUR RIFLES by C. W. Sawyer, a passage explains in detail the actions of a Civil War Marksman. A bench is constructed. The range to the target is verified with a theodolyte. The rifle is fired at a sighter target to get the exact windage and elevation settings for the powder charge employed. These verified settings are cranked in before the telling shot. This rifle was supported at the front by a foot that slid on a waxed block. The rear had set screws on a piece of metal for adjustment. All these actions sound familiar?

From where did these rifles and techniques come? Harvey Donaldson stated in 1949 there were heavy Turkey Match rifles, with scopes, in existence in the 1840's. Just as we see today, when the boys gather around for some friendly competition the advice to the gunsmith is, build the finest rifle, who cares that it's three months salary. In 1862 W.G. Langdon, a Boston watch and clock maker, and expert rifleman, was contracted by the government for 20 sniper rifles complete with telescope. His price was $150 each. The Governments on both sides of the conflict put out a call for the match rifles and skills of the general populace to be used by the sniper teams. The turkey rifle I've seen is a fully rested 37 pound piece. A bracket on the fore end fitted into a front rest, the rear was shot off an adjustable rest. With a 25x full length scope, percussion lock, false muzzle, and bullet starter the turkey's head was in grave danger when a rifleman touched off the cap.

Fine rifles of the period often included a target in the rifle case showing the accuracy possible. There are no verifiable records but there must have been some superb shooting going on. Harry M. Pope guaranteed his rifles to group into two and one half inches at 200 yards. Compare this to the manufacturers in Britain, who as of 1883 had only one riflemaker that would guarantee all shots in a 3″ circle at 100 yards.

The most popular rifle events in the late 1800's, up to 1905, were the Shuetzen Rifle matches. It was possible to order a rifle and accessories from the masters like Harry M. Pope, George Schoyen, Norman Brockway and William Billingshurst. Be assured the rifle would be super accurate and of the highest quality workmanship. The technique of shooting the rifle was not passed on to the benchrest shooter. The things sent down were the need for experimentation and testing to find the perfect bullet and powder charge for the best groups. Shuetzen rifles were very temperamental, easily affected by humidity and temperature they formed the nucleus of knowledge for the old time rifle crank.

A few of these rifles had wondrous accuracy. The most famous of them all is the Pope-Ballard 32/40 that Chas. W. Rowland used on May 16, 1901 for his exquisite ten shot, blackpowder, group of .725″ at 200 yards. It took fifty years for the modern shooter, with the best equipment, to beat that sparkler. This rifle was shot with the forend resting on a wooden block, the rear was often held by hand or rested on another wooden block. Rowland stated the wooden block was not as accurate as the hand held shots. Vibration control and shot to shot variation must have been a factor, our modern sandbags would have done him a world of good. He had a crude way to return-to-battery, however without lateral support his combination wouldn't line up straight like a current return to battery rig. One very important lesson C.W. Rowland leaves us is the careful noting of wind, and conditions, and duplicating it on subsequent shots.

The great experimenter Franklin W. Mann created his "Shooting Gibralter" in the Fall of 1901. This was a machine rest devised to hold barreled actions steady during experiments. With a cement top, legs that extended 40″ into the ground and a muslin cover for a shooting tube Dr. Mann had a machine rest so steady there was no change of impact in three years. Most of Mann's shooting was to experiment with bullet flight. In his book, THE BULLETS FLIGHT, Dr. Mann made several references to groups shot off a rest. When he started his serious experimenting in August of 1894 there's reference to a 30 yard group of 1.75 inches. From then till the turn of the century Dr. Mann achieved several five and ten shot groups of one inch at 100 yards. The normal group was more in the one and a half to two inch range. Then, as now, the ever present flyer drove him to conniptions. By 1902 Dr. Franklin Mann finally got a shooter. He shot eleven groups, with a barrel called the "Bumblebee", that averaged .63″ at 100 yards. This was the twenty third barrel he tried on his Shooting Gibralter!

C. W. Rowland continued his efforts for many years. Like many experimenters of the era he corresponded freely with others pursuing the same goal. On May 26th, 1931 Mr. Rowland completed a 40 shot group at 100 yards. The 40 shots measured half an inch by half an inch center to center! Fired from a machine rest with a .32/40 Schoyen, Mr Rowland took more than one day to complete the target. The shots were only let go during calms on a windy day. A few shooters still try the same thing, some even try it during a match.

*Harvey Donaldson, Al Marciante, and W.J. Prescott were among the attendees at the Johnstown, NY benchrest match in 1947.*

Photos and information exist from early benchrest matches held at Lisbon Schuetzen Verein in Taftville, Connecticut. These three shot matches for score were held as often as three times a year, from the early 1930's, until the late 1940's. They were attended by such notables as Harry Pope, John Kaufman, and in the later years Ray Biehler, Samuel Clark Jr., and Harvey Donaldson. Samuel Clark Jr., who we know shot there in 1946, states in the first edition of THE ULTIMATE IN RIFLE PRECISION, published in 1949: "At the rest matches of a club where I had been a regular attendant for some years". Harvey Donaldson commented about his visit and their successful shooting: "This trip was well worth our while. It was like a shot in the arm, for it gave the fellows confidence that they could shoot in fast company, and thus gave them more confidence that they could put on a match on the home grounds and make a success of it." More about this later.

Philip Sharpe, author of COMPLETE GUIDE TO HANDLOADING, published the first edition of his work in 1937. His chapter on testing bullets shows in great detail the construction of solid benches for rest shooting. Sharpe was an advocate of resting on the forearm rather than the barrel as was much practiced at the time. He stated the knowledgeable rifleman shooting off sandbags would usually beat the machine rests then available. Philip Sharpe used the bench extensively for testing his high-power match loads. Unfortunately, nowhere does he tell the exact group sizes that resulted.

By 1941 much of the information and equipment need for smaller groups and aggregates was in place. Loading tools by the L.E. Wilson Company were generally available. Their bullet seaters, case trimmers, resizing dies, neck reamers, and primer pocket reamers look much as they do today. Versions of the .219 Donaldson Wasp, .22 Varminter (.22/250) and various 25 caliber reamers were in the hands of local gunsmiths. There was a spreading of the general knowledge of accurate rifles. (Charles Landis used 2000-3000 letters as the basis for his book TWENTY-TWO CALIBER VARMINT RIFLES.)

December 7, 1941 put a hammerlock on powder and bullet supplies for the next few years. In 1944 the first modern benchrest match with connections to today was fired. The Puget Sound Snipers Congress of Seattle, Washington organized an all comers event. Rests were permitted in a match determined by aggregate group size at 200 yards. These were important concepts we still follow today. It's easy to show only the best group from the previous months shooting; when every shot counts the results are something to be proud of. 37 Shooters vied for the Championship. The winner was Roy Meister with an aggregate of 2.235" for four 5-shot groups at 200 yards. Small group was 1.27" by Roy using a Wilson Arrow .220. Their "Sniper King" trophy is still being contested.

Following their lead W. Jennings Prescott of Machias, New York (interesting side note, W.J. Prescott lived in Machias, New York, near the St. Lawrence Seaway. Harvey Donaldson was an avid fisherman and often fished at Machias, Maine, on the Maine coast. Hence the sometimes confusion between the two and mix up in other histories.) organized a small benchrest match for varmint rifles. This event at Machias, New York, early in the summer of 1947, was such a success Harvey Donaldson of Fultonville, New York set up another. This milestone, scheduled for the Labor Day weekend, at the Pine Tree Rifle Club in Johnstown, New York was to become the organizational beginning of benchrest. At this match the Eastern Bench Rest Shooters Association, later to become the NBRSA, was formed. Harvey Donaldson was named as their first President, Colonel Townsend Whelen, Frank Hubbard, and Samuel Clark Jr. were also named as officers.

An active organization and the terrific shooting from that match created national interest in benchrest shooting. During the three day match 21 three shot groups were fired by the 28 competitors. While the three shot for score seems to be brought over from the Taftville, Connecticut events one feature of these matches was concurrent score and group shooting. Aggregate Winner was W.J. Prescott at .4843". The top five competitors used handmade bullets out of RCBS dies. Another important component was available!

Evolution took place rapidly during the next few matches. By the Dubois, Pennsylvania match on October 4th and 5th, 1947 the 200 yard

*Benchrest shooter Mike Walker is the father of the .222 Remington and the Remington 722 action.*

stage was a 5 shot affair. Small group at 200 yards was a 1.0625 by Marcy Prescott. In 1989 some shooters go a whole season without a handful of groups that big!

By the early 1950's the size of record groups had shrunk substantially. These were groups fired in competition, with moving backers. The moving backer verifies the number of shots in these tiny holes. Many of these groups would still be below the small groups shot today in an average registered match. Using a .250-3000 Paul Dinant shot a 5 shot, 100 yard, group of .1057" on May 21, 1950. Crawford Hollidge shot a 10 shot, 100 yard, group of .2677" on September 5, 1953. Both of these are fine groups. Where the shooters of yesterday were behind was at 200 yards. One of the reasons had to be because of the scopes they used. With todays 36X scopes there's much better resolution. The 15x, 20x and 24x scopes just couldn't be held as fine. Everything else aside Bill Guse used a .22-250 to shoot a 5 shot, 200 yard group of .3896" on May 7, 1950. This is a great group for 1950, but, in 1989 a winning 200 yard aggregate in good conditions could have three out of five groups that small!

The introduction of the .222 Remington on March 1, 1950 provided the mainstay of Benchrest shooters for the next twenty five years. Mike Walker had produced a superbly accurate combination that wrested the best groups out of the available equipment. Just like the PPC many years later, the .222 was a success from it's first outing.

Throughout the rest of the 1950's the level of ability and equipment kept increasing. Shooters shared hard won knowledge with whoever was interested in listening. Of course they also shared it with some who weren't interested in hearing it, some things never change. The prosperity which followed World War II gave many the time and money to participate fully in the nationwide growth in benchrest.

The individual record groups didn't decrease dramatically. What did decrease was the aggregate. Aggregate scores are a true measure of a rifles accuracy. Aggregate scores consist of a minimum of 25 aimed shots spread over a period of time; all the vagaries of wind and mirage have come into play. Any problems with the bench, or the rests, would have been exposed. Inconsistent ignition from improper components would reveal substandard cartridge design. Part of the decrease is from equipment and loads, part of the decrease has been from the riflemen realizing they have to get that last shot into a hole on every group.

The aggregate has indeed been slipping. The 100 yard varmint record for five 5-shot groups steadily dropped to Lynn Hunts record of .2189 shot on July 12, 1964. Think about that. Five groups, each with five shots, all averaging under 1/4 inch.

By 1981 that had nose dived to below two tenths of an inch. Harvey Miller, Larry Earp, Seely Masker, Pat McMillan and many others had easily shattered that barrier. Today it is easy to see scores that just yesterday were an impossibility. Harvey Donaldson wouldn't know what to think about a fibreglass stocked 6PPC capable of a .125″ five shot group at 200 yards. We've come a long way.

History is an amazing thing. Those who fully participated in it, and know all the answers, are not available to verify information. Specifically, the fact of the earliest organized benchrest matches. The earliest turkey shoots held ever since the middle 1840's were often contested with the rifle resting on a log. There were several events such as participated in by C.W. Rowland in the 1930's which can't be called organized events. A group got together through word of mouth, held a one day event, and then went their merry way. Believing the need for the recognized earliest benchrest matches to be advertised, annual events, the author believes the first benchrest matches were fired at the Lisbon Schuetzen Verein, in Taftville, Connecticut. These events from the early 1930's to the late 1940's were fired from a rest, three shots for score at 100 yards. Both blackpowder Schuetzen rifles firing lead bullets, and modern varmint rifles firing jacketed bullets were shot from a rest.

# 3

# *The Rifle*

The individual pieces which make up a modern benchrest rifle were not discovered by accident. Testing, trial and error, and more testing have given us the components for the most accurate rifles in the world. Every accuracy record for group size out to 1000 yards was shot by a benchrest style rifle. At 100 yards the existing five shot record is under 1/32 MOA. Amazing.

Many combinations of the available equipment might all lead to world class accuracy. To make a qualified decision about what components to use in building your next rifle let's look at the different pieces.

## Stocks

The purpose of the stock is to hold the barreled action rigidly without using up too much of the allotted weight for the class in which the rifle is being used. At the same time the stock must retain its shape during the act of firing. Early benchrest rifles were made with wood stocks. Using the available military actions, with their poor bedding surface, rifles had to be rebedded as often as every day. Laminated wood eliminated some of the stability problems, but laminated stocks were heavy unless eggshelled (hollowed out butt and forend). Any hunter who has done much traveling knows that even the most inert piece of laminated wood can move during changes in humidity and temperature; the one piece stock made from a nicely figured piece of wood is much worse.

It was the advent of the foam filled fibreglass stock which kicked benchrest rifles out of the wood era. The first fibreglass stock used in competition was a three piece affair made by Jerry Rogers, he shot the gun to victory in the 1967 and 1968 Nationals. The road to the success of the breed started when Chet Brown and Lee Six, among others, developed the

*Benchrest stocks allow creativity not available on hunting rifle stocks. Ron Parker's rifle sports a delightful Rodney Hutcherson paint job.*

rigid lightweight stock we use today. Chet found out the expansion rate of fibreglass was close to the expansion rate of steel. After much experimentation they discovered a two piece mold with the halves joined together later made the most sense for their initial testing. Hundreds of hours were spent on molds, mold releases, cure time, mixes and various other bits of the problem. Testing showed the hollow fibreglass stock would shoot good groups, but only if the guard screws were loose, the hollow bedding area wouldn't stand up to the tightening procedure some in the field deemed necessary. Like anything else which is against the norm, public acceptance took a while in coming. It was the hollow feel, and the ringing tap which caused the most shooter worry. When Chet and Lee filled the hollow stock with Polyurethane foam; conventional bedding techniques, and screw tension which everyone understood, worked again. By 1971 fibreglass stocks from the shop were showing up at a few matches, and doing quite well. Like anything else, a new product gets snickered at till it pastes a few good scores on the wall, then everyone wants one. Later refinements came in the form of glue-in bedding. It might not be any better than conventional bedding, but it sure is easier to do. While Lee and Chet were working on release agents they, along with anyone else doing the same thing, had some unintentional glue-ins when the release agent didn't work, or was accidently left off. With the action epoxy bonded directly to the stock the age old problem of the bedding getting solvent soaked, and softening up, has been almost entirely eliminated. There's still a chance that some of our solvents can damage the bedding, but with a solid bottomed action and a long bore guide it's not likely.

The use of lightweight fibreglass, Kevlar, and graphite in rifle stocks has allowed the beefing up of the other rifle components. By starting with a Kevlar or graphite stock it's easy to use a heavy barrel, and a heavy action, in Heavy Varmint. The light stocks are more of an advantage in the 10 1/2 pound classes. A one and a half pound Light Varmint stock allows a stout barrel and action, a definite accuracy enhancer.

The advent of aftermarket drop-in or factory synthetic stocks for our everyday hunting rifles has made the use of rifles in varying amounts of moisture acceptable without constant re-sighting in. Free floated sporting weight tubes give some amazing accuracy when an accurized action is mated to a suitable stock.

## Actions

The action is the building block on which the rifle is assembled. Comprised of a hollow receiver, the trigger assembly, and a bolt, future accuracy potential starts out on the right foot with an accurized action. Since it's the foundation, squareness of all the angles, and trueness of all the lines gains importance. Long ago the battle for recognition as the most accurate type of action was won hands down by the turning bolt family. Autoloading, lever action, falling block, and break top types all have their champions, as each has a specific use.

The prime advantages for the bolt action stem from its basic rigidity, both in the action and in its bedding into the stock, and it's positive breeching which supplies the same cartridge support for the first, and subsequent, shots. Recent experimentation has led to the development of some very accurate rifles based on the M16. An accurized M16 is capable of being more accurate than most out of the box turning bolt guns, only it's not as accurate as the custom bolt action benchrest rifles. The gas guns will shoot groups approaching greatness, but a fifth shot thrown .200″ from a .200″ four shotter still leaves a hole of .400″. In the competitive game today there can't be any shots thrown that are the rifles fault.

Since the first Mauser was produced for the military in the last century there haven't been any startling revelations in the action world. What we've done in the last hundred years is learn the parameters which get the most performance out of the equipment. In 1949, benchrest rifles were mostly made on the Mauser 98 action. Then, as now, if something is plentiful, and cheap, there will be lots of them in use. Mausers had been designed for military use, there were a few things shooters discovered that needed changing. The generous magazine cut, and loading port, didn't leave much meat to stiffen the action. With a heavy barrel sticking downrange there

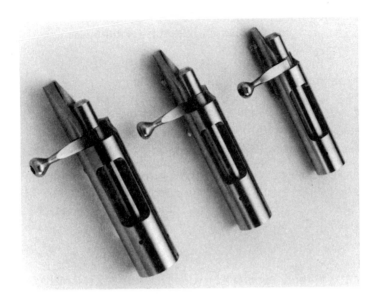

*Hall actions are one of the benchrest shooters favorites. Here the line up includes the Model B, the Model M, and the standard.*

wasn't enough bedding surface to get away with full floating the tube, the small bedding area was highly stressed and required frequent rebedding. Adding in the stone-ax paced firing pin fall did anything but decrease group size. Various attempts to stiffen the action helped, sleeves were being tried by the middle 1950's, but something was still lacking. Shortfalls in the equipment at hand caused a few men with machinist backgrounds to make their own actions.

The early custom actions, available over the years in quantities ranging anywhere from a few to several hundred, included the Hart, John Dewey and Shilen, Charles Williams and his Benchmaster, Sherman and his Superior, Clarence Detsch, Ralph Stolle, Baucher, Tirrell, McMillan, Ferris Pindell and Homer Culver. Mostly these independent operators found the amount of work to produce the tolerances required meant it wasn't economically feasible to make actions for resale. Since the era of the small one man shop which put out just a few actions there have been several small companies who have continued, and built up a livelihood in action making.

Robert W. Hart & Son of Nescopeck, Pennsylvania has been in the action business for many years. With the longest continuous run of custom action making they have consistently produced exact actions which result in accurate rifles. Their six models include the light weight No. 1 at 2 lb. 9 oz., the No. 1A at 3 lb. 14 oz., all the way to the heavyweight, 15 1/2" long, No. 4.

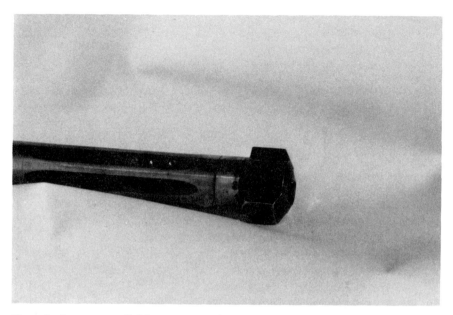

*Cone bolts are available on several of the custom actions. The matching angle in the end of the barrel helps speed up the firing rate.*

Depending of the weight of the other components Hart makes an action which easily fits any accuracy requirement.

Ed Shilen made his first two actions during the winter of 1960. They were accurate, won a slew of matches, other shooters were willing to plunk down cash for them, the die was cast. In the ensuing years there were several changes in location, from Dryden, New York, where the first 100 or so actions were made, to Clinton Corners, New York (during an association with SS&D) where the next 162-170 actions were made. In 1966 Ed Shilen moved his business to the Gulf Coast. Shilen Rifles, Inc. is currently based in Ennis, Texas where they offer three actions to the accuracy buff. The DGA/BP-S is a single shot which weighs a scant 1 lb. 15 oz. Slightly longer and heavier at 2 lb. 4 oz. is the DGA/BP which is the usual choice for 10 1/2 pound guns. Heavy Varmint, Silhouette and super accurate varmint/small game rifles get built on the largest action he makes, the three pound DGA.

Hall Mfg. was started in 1977 by Allan Hall. With over 20 years experience in designing and building actions Allan started with the best of his ideas, the best of materials, and built his idea of the best actions. Made from the same 17-4 stainless steel that's used in the landing gear of jet planes Hall actions are highly resistant to any of the rust and corrosion problems exhibited by steel or aluminum actions. The four different Hall actions include the 1 lb. 15 oz. Standard Action, the Model M at 2 lb. 10 oz., and the big Model B for Heavy Bench and maximum weight Heavy

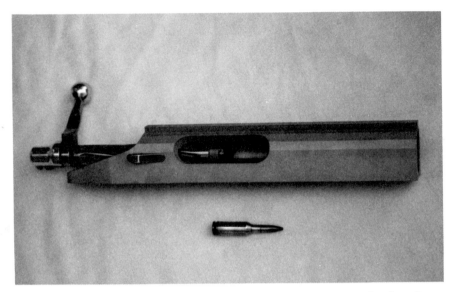

*Stolle actions have become the most popular custom action for benchrest rifles. Well made and beautiful rifles are the conclusion when a Stolle is used.*

Varmint rifles at 3 lb. 10 oz. For the biggest of those super big boomers, designed for 1000 yard benchrest or long range hunting, Hall Mfg. has just released the Express Action. With a port 3 7/16″ long the action handles the long 378 Weatherby case. Both solid bottom and repeaters are available in the Express.

Ralph and Eldon Stolle combined some machining tricks with the popular idea of increasing bedding surface area, and stiffness, by sleeving a steel action in aluminum. They decided to go the idea one better, by making a one piece action from several pieces. This very popular action combined the best of both worlds. There was a large, lightweight, outside surface for accurate bedding, and there was steel at all of the bearing points. Ralph Stolles' death several years ago left the production of Stolle actions to George Kelbly. Four actions are available, the Panda, Polar, Kodiak, and Teddy are ready to fill whatever needs are presented.

Mo DeFina of MCS Inc. purchased the action making machinery of CPS. The original CPS was a well made, and accurate, action based on a two part steel/aluminum configuration similar to the one used in the Stolle. They took a round steel core and heat fit a drilled aluminum block over it. (There's seven seconds to get the aluminum from the oven and press the frozen steel tube into it; get it together correctly the first time - or else!) Though well made, CPS never constituted a significant force atop the leader board. Several shooters, Bob White and I among them, set a number of records, and won a bunch of big matches. It was poor business sense, multiple promises on items which were never delivered, and in general, pissing off anyone who came in contact with the company which caused the majority of the benchrest group to give them a wide berth. The changeover to MCS as the supplier caused an instant turn around in availability, and desirability of the action for accuracy work.

Wichita Arms, Inc. of Wichita, Kansas makes an action which is the favorite of some of the countries hottest shooters. The Wichita WBR 1375 is 2 lb. 10 oz, 8″ long, with a three locking lug cone bolt, and an option of opposite bolt/loading port. Rifles built on this action are strong and fast.

Touching on the custom actions brings up the debt benchrest shooters and the accuracy minded rifleman owe to Mike Walker and Remington Arms. This combination produced the first Remington Model 722, a commercial action with all the potential to win without having to build a custom. They had picked up the gauntlet, and worked on improving the product offered to the benchrest shooter, when none of the other manufacturers showed any interest. With its good bedding area, stiffness, and fast lock time the 722 quickly became the commercial favorite of the benchrester. Not resting on its laurels, over time, Remington developed the 40X specifically for accuracy work. The diameter was beefed up, the loading port was shrunk, and the magazine cut was removed. The increased stiffness from these changes allowed any barrel to be full floated without damaging the bedding. During the 1970's it was the 40X which formed the bulk of the accurate rifles on any firing line. A 40X can still be made into a superbly accurate rifle in the late 1980's. With so many fine custom actions available the practice has fallen by the wayside.

Most 40X rifles makeing the line today are there because the owner had one in the closet when the benchrest bug bit. In order to bring it up to top standards there are a few things which have to be done to remove the commercial tolerances, and their resultant damage to group size. Where custom actions are crafted one at a time by someone who isn't willing to sacrifice perfection, the Remington 40X and its cousins the XP100, Model 600, and Model 700 need to be trued. The lugs must be lapped into full contact, the recoil shoulders need to be cleaned up, the receiver face must be cleaned up, the threads must be checked for straightness, and fixed if necessary. With the level of competition where it is today you can't go to the line with only half the work done. When the whole job is completed you'll find that the cost of the action ($300.00) and the money spent to fix it to perfection (another $200.00 to $300.00) comes up to almost the cost of a new custom action.

With up to 17% of the earths population shooting from the left side they have no choice but to buy a made-to-order action. Here's another kicker that should sway the decision towards a custom. When it comes time to sell the rifle there's a significant difference in the resale value. With the line comprised of 80% hand-crafted actions shooters tend to look down their nose a little at rifles based on the 40X. There might not be any difference in the accuracy potential, that's just the way the human race operates.

## Barrels

A bullet in the correct place on the target is the goal for each shot we liberate. Dr. Mann's experiments at the turn of the century proved the importance of delivering a bullet into flight with as little deformation as possible. It's the job of the barrel to see that for every shot, the bullet is sent in good shape, and on the same line. In order to excel at its task a rifle barrel must have a straight hole, a uniform size, and an excellent finish.

Benchrest quality barrels are produced using either of two methods for rifling. These are cut rifling, and button rifling. Cut rifling is the more historic of the two. The excellent barrel makers of the Shuetzen period used the process to produce barrels which were the most accurate in the world. Gregoire produced the best benchrest barrels in the world from the late 1940's up to 1955. Gregoire barrels at the time had a problem with longevity. It was a common statement that as soon as an accurate load for the barrel was worked up the barrel was "washed out". Ed Shilens' recent tests on an original, unfired, Gregoire barrel showed it to be made out of a "dirty" chrome-moly steel. Dirty means there's foreign substance in the steel, as the rifle is fired these compounds burn out, and leave pits in the barrel. Accuracy suffers when the pits pick up jacket material and fouling. The barrels weren't washing out, they were victims of the available steel. A good barrel is the product of correct machining technique, if Gregoire and the early custom makers had access to our high quality stainless they would have been able to produce a barrel which would be competitive today.

During World War II Mike Walker and Remington developed the "button" process. A steel slug with the shape of the grooves and lands on it was pulled through the lubricated barrel; imparting its shape to the surrounding steel. By 1948 Mike was using match barrels he had made, around 1953- 1954 he helped set up the initial Hart barrel business with Clyde and Charlie Hart. They proved the button process would turn out accurate barrels. Refinements over the years changed the steel button into carbide, numerous other changes improved consistency. Like any operation, 35 years of doing the same thing showed the little tricks which improved the end product.

Since the era of the early 1950's, when Gregoire used chrome-moly, it's been proven that suitable stainless gives a much longer accuracy life, in the .222 up to twice as long. The steel used in modern barrels must have high tensile strength to withstand the pressures developed in our high- intensity cartridges. It must be free from defects, it must be machinable, steel that's difficult to work means the end product won't be suitable. The cleaner the

*Paul J. Hart was one of the sports early dominators. P.J. had as many as three IBS Championship plaques over his mantle at one time.*

steel, the fewer pits appear as the foreign substance burns out, the longer the accuracy life.

Finish lapping provides the final surface to decrease fouling. Correctly done button rifled barrels are consistent to within .0001″ to .0002″ across the groove diameter for the entire length of the barrel. We know the most accurate bullet is one that moves through the barrel in a smooth, even, push as the burning gasses expand. It makes sense that a rifle with exact dimensions, a smooth finish, and uniform rifling pitch from one end to the other should deliver the bullet the most consistently. The most accurate barrel in the world can't perform up to snuff unless it's installed on a good action, correctly chambered and crowned. Saving a few dollars by going to an amateur gunsmith just because they're local will cost in the long run. Benchrest quality chambering work on a match grade barrel isn't all that difficult for someone who's willing to do it right. Just make sure it's done right!

When you take delivery of that new "hummer" which you think just might get you into the Hall of Fame, a little patience, and the proper break in will ensure you and your new hummer get off on the right foot. 20 years ago the rest of the equipment, and the skills of the shooter, weren't up to proving the final bit of accuracy which was available in a rifle barrel. The day has come where that's the case so use the "one shot and clean" break in method for a new barrel. Fire the first shot, clean with Shooters Choice,

*Frank Calicchia shows off his .186" 200 yard group. Proving the old saying that nice guys don't always finish first; this wasn't the small group of the match.*

then Sweets 7.62 Solvent, then Shooters choice. If the Sweets doesn't show any copper, patch out and fire another shot. Repeat the one shot and clean till the Shooters Choice doesn't show any fouling. An average would be five to seven shots, though sometimes it takes longer. Then shoot some three shot groups and clean. If the patches look ok you're all set. A bit of care early in the barrels life will decrease copper fouling as time goes on. There's been some debate about the value of this process. So great an authority as Jack Sutton (who works in the Hart Rifle Barrel shop) says fireforming with two ten shot groups, and a thorough cleaning after each is all that's necessary.

Super accuracy for any of the available barrels is only in the 1500 round range. Good barrels show competitive accuracy up to 2000-2500 rounds. After that we're fooling ourselves by thinking the rifle is still in top shape, it might win a 20 shooter local match, but it won't cut the mustard at the Super Shoot. Install another barrel and use the old one for practice on windy days where there's two inches of wind drift.

There are two easy ways to keep track of the number of shots through a barrel. First is to keep every target the barrel has ever fired. At the end of the year count up every shot on the targets and write the number down. It takes a while but the information is valuable; don't forget the practice targets. The second is the method I use, get a separate primer tray for each rifle you'll shoot during the season. Every time you dump another 100 primers

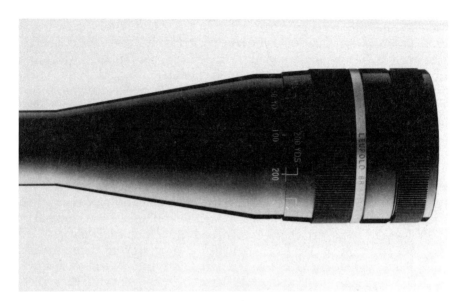

*Since the introduction of the 24X and 36X: Leupold scopes have been on more benchrest rifles than any other brand. The new BR 24X and BR 36X with their locking adjustable objective should continue their dominance.*

into the tray mark it down on the master sheet in your shooting box. Keeping track this way saves the hour it takes to count shots on the targets. You never forget to include the practice shots. Ever notice how there's never been a used benchrest rifle for sale which has more than 1000 rounds through it? More people than will admit it don't keep track of the number of rounds through a barrel. The only way to find a great barrel is to take one out and shoot it! Keep looking and testing, for they're there to be found.

For a more complete explanation of the barrel making process look at a copy of THE ACCURATE RIFLE and review the comments by Clyde Hart and Ed Shilen.

### Rifle Telescopes

A benchrest rifle might be the most accurate in the world, but if we didn't have the resolution from a high powered scope there's no way to find out if that's the case.

The short, internally adjusted, scopes introduced since 1970 have been a significant improvement over the long, externally adjusted, scopes which were available till then. These new scopes have removed 20% from the size of the average group, they along with the PPC, have been rated as the most important reasons for the recent decline in aggregate sizes. When combined with the increase in scope power there's better target resolution and a decrease in scope induced errors. Early in the sports history there was a general agreement that 30X was too much magnification for benchrest shooting (call it common knowledge - misguided, but common). Crawford Hollidge commented in 1962 that with higher than 25X you couldn't read the mirage. In the early 1970's Warren Page still claimed that anything over 30X was wasted, he thought you needed a wide field of view to watch what was going on at your neighbors target, and to see what the conditions were up to down range.

The advent of the Redfield 3200, Lyman LWBR series, and the Leupold 24X were enough to shake up the status quo and get people thinking about changing to a higher power. Wally Siebert would boost the power of the Lyman scopes for any who were interested. With the short scopes mounted entirely on the receiver the era of the switch barrel gun was opened. The older Unertl, Fecker, Litschert, Lyman, and Redfield scopes were installed with the front mount on the barrel. These mounts with their exposed adjustments and spring returns were a haven for misalignment. One speck of dust under one of the adjusting legs was enough to move a shot. Calculations show us that just .001″ of movement at the rifle translates into 1/4″ at the 100 yard target. No wonder it's so tough to shoot offhand!

Benchrest shooters are never easily satisfied. They were requesting both short scopes and light weight. To get these scopes short and light the manufacturers had to make a trade off somewhere. The only place to take off weight was to make the tubes thinner, and the internal mechanism as small and light as possible. These smaller and lighter parts are more easily effected by wear or damage than stouter parts. The trade off to a lighter weight tube brings us to some important considerations. Most benchrest shooters don't click the scope adjustments in the middle of a group. If it's necessary to change the windage during a group shoot one or two sighter shots to settle the adjustments before firing another record shot. Scopes are designed to take great amounts of front and rear loading. They are not designed to take any lateral deflection, or twisting. The easiest way to change point of impact is to carry the rifle by its scope, or use the scope bell as a leverage point when you're lifting a sticky bolt. When you need leverage move your thumb to the mount, which is rigid enough to take the side loads.

Scopes go bad in one of two forms, they either drop off gradually, flipping a shot once in a while, or they go to pot all at once, and can't hit the broad side of a barn. It's difficult to know when the first problem is cropping up. Unless you're shooting during perfect conditions a shot out by 1/4″ is usually attributed to the conditions. I had a problem with a scope at the beginning of the season two years ago. Job pressures kept me from getting as much testing and practice as was usually the case at the beginning of a year. A full match schedule was planned, it included long distance travel to the Cactus in Phoenix, the Crawfish in Lafayette, Louisiana, and the Super

*A nice scope helps complete a rifle. Here Dr. Richard Maretzo shows off another way to spruce up the old shooting iron. His "Bet A Martini" rifle has accounted for several big match wins. Next to it: two rifles from the shop of Jim Greenawalt put some snap into the benchrest line.*

Shoot in Ohio. In Phoenix I was having a terrible time getting good groups, but put it down to windy conditions, and being rusty at the first match of the year. The Crawfish showed the same trouble getting a good group. Shooting next to Jim Hostettler, there was the identical problem of vertical shots out of the group when the flags pointed to them dropping right in. Having trouble during conditions much better than in Phoenix I started to wonder what the problem was. It's not fun finishing 75th two matches in a row when you're trying to win.

Work kept me from shooting again till the Super Shoot. The first day the same thing kept cropping up. Those baffling moments where a high or low shot would take a .150″ group to .375″. By the end of the second day I was beside myself with frustration. One nice thing about the Super Shoot, it's so well organized there's always several hours the end of the day where you can shoot groups, right up till dark. Those loading with me didn't want to stay and shoot, a steak in Canal Fulton was calling their name, so I started loading different combinations of powder and seating depth. Shooting in a breeze at 200 yards the groups were above .750″ no matter which combination was thrown together. When the wind started to die down, closer to dusk, the groups didn't get any smaller. Those shooting at nearby benches were getting .300″ and .400 inch efforts and the ones in front of my rifle were stuck on .750″. Knowing for sure there was something wrong I begged a scope of known ability off John Jones. The first group with it, right at dusk, was a .400″. Three big matches and over $1000.00 in travel expenses later the problem was corrected. Placings of 26th and 116th from the first two days became placings of 11th and 6th after switching scopes. Don't be a dummy, learn from your mistakes, switch to a known scope if there's a chance it's the bogey man. Luckily the manufacturers stand behind their products. The problem with the scope turned out to be slack in the objective lens and the manufacturer replaced the whole scope free of charge.

The most popular scope for benchrest has been the Leupold 36X. Its major flaw was the lack of a locking ring on the parallax adjustment. With the introduction of the new BR 24X and BR 36X this fault won't trouble us any more. They're still the only scope in the price range which doesn't come through with lens covers. An oversight that any owner of a scope should correct immediately. Always cover the scope with a lens cap, or rag, before brushing solvent through the bore. When the bristle brush exits the end of the barrel it flings a mist of tiny solvent droplets into the air. Not something you want on the fluoride coating of your scope lens.

Setting up a rifle with a new scope is easy, there are a few handy hints which might make things easier. First item of business is to set up the bases and mounts parallel to the bore. Use high quality bases which were designed to fit the receiver. Install the rings as instructed by the manufacturer, some rings have built in adjustment, they're designed to be installed in relation to each other, otherwise the scope will be out of line. Check the scope adjustments and make sure the crosshairs are centered in their range of travel. The best optics in a scope are in the center, that's where we want the aiming point to be when we're all done. With the scope loosely installed gently snug up the screws on the rings. Bore sight to see if the crosshairs are close to the indicated point of impact. Some rings, like the Bushnell lightweights, can be reversed if the scope is out of line: read the instructions for which way to rotate the rings depending on where you need to move the scope. After everything checks out, mark the rings with a file to show which ring, and top goes together and in which position. Make a single file mark across the right hand side of the two part front ring, and two file cuts across the right hand side of the back ring. A fancy step at this point is to lap or bed the rings. Done wrong lapping can damage the rings, so I'll ask you to have someone show you the correct way. If you're a machinist, or have a friend who can help with the work, machine your own blocks and rings, get everything matched and on the centerline. Scopes become interchangeable if everything is straight.

Once the scope is tightened down in the rings it's time to start adjusting the optics. First - read the manufacturers instructions. Second - proceed with focusing the eyepiece. When the eyepiece is focused so the crosshairs are as sharp and as black as possible lock the ring, it's time to remove the parallax by using the adjustable objective. Hunting scopes don't need

*Canadian Vic Swindlehurst has just finished adjusting his scope and gets ready to commence a record string.*

adjustable objective lenses, minute amounts of parallax aren't enough to cause a problem in the field. In the case of high class target rifles it's imperative to get out the parallax before shooting from the bench. Set the rifle on a steady front and rear rest. Ignoring the figures stamped on the ring, adjust the objective back and forth till the target seems to be at its crispest. Then, with the crosshairs right next to a line on the target, slowly wiggle your head side to side in the field of view, if the crosshairs move on the target there's more parallax to be taken out. Make a minute adjustment in the objective and wiggle your head again. Keep at it till there's no movement in the crosshairs. Anytime there's a yardage change the process will have to be repeated. On days where there's lots of mirage running, move the ring to your standard point, then see if you can get the image any sharper, it's impossible to get a perfect sight picture with all that influence from the mirage.

Add a mirage shield: rifle barrels heat up as shots are fired and the heat transfers to the air directly in the line of sight. If we don't divert the rising heat waves our sight picture will be distorted by barrel mirage. The heat waves rising off the barrel have no bearing on any of the conditions downrange, and cause some gosh-awful shots. Mirage shields can be plastic tubes manufactured specifically for the type of scope you use, or simple pieces of target material taped onto the front of the scope. With paper, tape them in a "U" shape from the front of the scope and extend them to within one inch of the muzzle. Lester Bruno and I seem to have a contest to see who can have the rattiest mirage shield. A ripped piece of target attached with a chunk of masking tape doesn't look as neat as Gary Ocock's carefully fitted and trimmed shade. Now let's get ready to bore sight.

The ability to bore sight, then get a rifle sighted in quickly, is a maneuver every rifleman should have in their bag. The keenest trick in bore sighting is to set up the rifle on steady sand bags, then look through the bore from three feet behind the rifle. Getting the bull centered in the bore isn't difficult when you're not craning your neck like a giraffe trying for water. Trick number two is something everyone should know. After the first shot impacts the target, realign the sights on the aiming point, keep the rifle absolutely steady and carefully use the scope adjustments to move the point of aim to the point of impact. What do you know, two shots and you're sighted in, another feat that was easy because the rifle was set on solid bags and a bench. That trick makes you a hero during deer season. Deer chasers, who have already wasted two boxes of 30-30 ammo, will whistle when it's only two shots for a knowledgeable rifleman. Shooters who seem to know something always attract those who wonder what's going on, and need help. Some of the things are surprisingly simple, but without hands on experience the shooter can't put their finger on the problem. I was sighting in a hunting rifle one year when two boys with a lever action asked if I could help get them on paper. They said: "The shots were low and we kept cranking up and up and now we're not even on the paper". Looking at their rig they had the scope rotated 90 degrees. The left to right adjustment knob was on the top, the vertical adjustment knob was on the left side. No wonder they couldn't get sighted in. When they cranked on the knob marked up, it moved point of impact to the left. Sure gets confusing sometimes when you think you're following the directions.

For those times at 200 or 300 yards when a bullet doesn't want to punch a hole where you can find it there's a ruse you can pull to get on easily. Enlist a buddy as a spotter. Pick out a rock or a dirt clod on the backstop - make sure you're both looking at the same spot! Even if the shot hits several feet from the clod your spotter can say two feet left, six inches up, and you'll be on the paper in a hurry. If you're all set, and notice the new shooter beside you is having trouble, speak up and volunteer to be a spotter before they use all the shots in their block, besides being a hero you'll save the line the frustration of waiting for more cases to be reloaded.

For a scope which is switched between rifles, or for a switch barrel gun, write down the scope settings so next time out the rifle is close before the first shot.

A handy item appeared a few years ago for the shooter who had an accident, or is losing the eyesight in their dominant eye. After many years mounting a rifle to one shoulder it's uncomfortable to switch over to the other side. Alvin Davidson supplies an offset scope mount which allows a right hander to shoot with the scope in front of the left eye. If you've ever seen anyone trying to shoot a cross over stock (where the buttstock is cut away so they can get their left eye to the scope) you know this is a handy device. For a paltry $50.00 Davidson has a seven ounce rig which could extend your pleasure for years.

*Mel Estep, who proves that sometimes nice guys do finish first, shows his style on the way to the firing line.*

# 4

# *The 6PPC*

The 6PPC is the most important cartridge introduced to the accuracy minded shooter since the 1950 release of the .222 Remington. In late 1974 Dr. Louis Palmisano and Ferris Pindell finished designing the PPC series. Lou had done most of the design work, and Ferris used his skills as a master machinist to turn the ideas into reality. Like the .222, the PPC series was an instant competitive success. From the first big victories in the 1975 Super Shoot, by the 22 PPC, to today where 95% of all shooters on the line use a 6PPC, the design has become the cartridge to beat.

Dr. Palmisano and Ferris Pindell scientifically experimented for a new design. They checked all the existing base cases for adaptability. Tests led them to believe a smaller flash hole would be helpful for extreme accuracy. In the normal .081″ primer hole a small rifle primer will reliably ignite an inch and a half of powder, but if there's a smaller primer hole it will ignite up to an inch and three quarters. Al Angerman's test of effect of flash hole size on primer flash showed a slight decreasing of length, diameter, and volume of flash as the flash hole diameter decreased. There's an apparent contradiction here but Dr. Palmisano spent lots of greenbacks with Dan Pawlak proving it.

Ferris and Lou heard of a case with the attributes they were looking for. This case was the .220 Russian: a running boar cartridge from the Soviet Union. The .220 Russian was derived from the 7.62 X 39mm as used in the AK-47. This new case had a flash hole of .066″ and used a small rifle primer; experiments soon proved they had a winner. It's ironic, a case designed for spraying the landscape and hitting things every once in a while became the basis for the cartridge which holds all but a couple of the worlds accuracy records out to 300 yards.

*The creator of the PPC, Lou Palmisano, gets ready to punch another one hole group with his accurate little number.*

Thorough ballistic lab testing by the late Dan Pawlak found this cartridge to have an extremely uniform pressure/time ratio. Even a poor benchrest rifle can achieve target strings with less than 30 to 40 foot per second velocity variation between the shots. Since a rifle barrel vibrates in an oval when fired the smallest possible variation is usually more accurate. I have to say usually here; several people have tried to load for accuracy by checking only the fps spread. Some loads with 15 fps variation haven't been as accurate as those with 50. With a PPC Allie Euber has shot strings with ZERO deviation, every shot had exactly the same velocity. Somewhere in the middle is where the accurate loads usually end up. I try to keep the variation to less than 50 fps.

Base cases for the PPC are made by SAKO of Finland. With good wall thickness uniformity and two parts per million silver in its brass formula, the case performs well. Their brass formula and the slight semi-balloon head design of the .220 Russian case cause the cases to flow slightly more than a comparable .222 would. This flow is no big thing for the shooter, the small primer pocket leaves plenty of brass in the case head to withstand pressure. With a bench rest rifles tight necked or neck sized cases only needing full length resizing every 10-20 firings (depending on the pressure of the load) the brass work hardens much more slowly than a full length resized case would. Testing shows one of the common causes for case lengthening is full length resizing, then dragging the case over a tight

*From the left: .222 Remington, .22BR, 6PPC, and a .243 for comparison.*

expander button. With neck sizing it's common for a shooter to get from 50 to 150 firings from a case when shot with reasonable loads.

The 6PPC has many offspring. The .22 PPC was introduced first, campaigned and advertised heavily; though not nearly so successful as the 6PPC. The longer and shorter PPC derivatives include the .22 Waldog, 6MM Texan (I wonder where he lives?) 6PPCL, 6AGG, 6 Hex, and many others. All adjust the basic case design, just a little here, a scootch there, other than the Waldog by Dan Dowling most have only a few promoters. Even the original designers have continued to work on new cases. Ferris Pindell at last count was up to twenty different designs since the PPC. Dr. Palmisano has introduced several long PPC variations; mostly developed for the US Olympic team. He recently stated he was about to spend more time at the shooting bench and less time fiddling with new ideas. We can only hope Lou keeps at least one project on the burner all the time.

David Brennan, Editor of PRECISION SHOOTING Magazine has been instrumental in creating enthusiasm for continued wildcat research. He instigated and agitated till Hugh Reed and the Federal Cartridge Corporation came through with a run of 30 American brass. The 30 American is a 30-30 standard case, annealed further down the case, with a small primer and flash hole. Federal used their target tolerances during this order; case wall thickness is remarkably consistent. That original 50,000 case order was gobbled up and another 50,000 are on order. To use that quantity there must have been lots of resizing lube and midnight oil being burned somewhere. Using the Remington URBR base case (.308 small primer) I've developed my own case called the .257 Aggwhacker. At 1.610″, suitable for a .308 sized bolt, the case shoots as well as the bullets available for it. As this was produced to be a few percent less wind sensitive than the 6PPC it would get shot when the wind is howling across the range. The 6PPC, with superb handmade benchrest bullets, if steered right, can shoot tiny groups in a howling wind, so not much has been gained. Until match quality jackets become available for any caliber other than .22 or 6mm nothing else stands a chance. Theoretical advantages don't do any good till the equipment is available to take the advantages from the scratch pad to the firing line. Much of the fun from creating a case is cerebral stimulation, just like in school the way to learn something is to dive in with both feet. Unfortunately, at the same time your feet get wet the checkbook takes a soaking!

Creighton Audette states his and others research has proven it's not entirely the shape of the case that provides consistent ignition and accuracy. It's the case as a whole and how it acts and reacts with the other components. The relationship with the primer, primer hole size, primer flash, case volume, powder type, powder charge, burning rate, bullet jump, engraving resistance, and bearing surface. The PPC has been well matched, all these items act in concert to produce fine results. It sets up easily with many different combinations of primer, powder, and bullet. The powders in constant use by competitive shooters are Hodgdon's H322, Thunderbird T322, T32, and Norma 201. Many loads in a very broad range will shoot good groups. Depending on the barrel length, bullet weight, and powder charge, bullet velocity can be anywhere from 3050 fps to almost 3500 fps. My favorite loading is 27.8 to 28.2 grains of H322 behind a 68 grain Bruno Boat Tail Bullet .010″ off the lands, ignited by a Federal 205 M primer. Several other powders with a similar burning rate have been tried. Tom Horenburg of Staten Island used 3031 for one summer: it shot well for him but the grains are too long for consistent powder measure metering. Torbjorn Haggblom of Finland used 25 grains of IMR 4198 to shoot a .082″ group at 100 meters. That's an impressive group, but 4198's relative burning rate is a little quick for the 6PPC, it's not possible to get 100% loading density in the normal pressure range. Dennis Wagner of Bethany, Oklahoma as well as Red Cornelison of Seminole, Oklahoma still have a supply of the old BLC 1, it hasn't been manufactured since ten years before I was wearing short pants. Asking Dennis where he got it, he said: "a little here, a little there". A few people have tried Hodgdon H335, W-W 748, the discontinued Hercules RelodeR #7, and RelodeR #11 all without sustained success.

To show how changes in case volume can have a big difference in the accuracy potential we have only to look at how the parent .220 Russian case performs in a benchrest rifle. One year I shot next to the late Glenn Price

*Though the PPC wins most of the big events other cartridges win their share. Glenn Newick shows off several awards won with the help of a 6BR.*

several times during the summer matches. He had been shooting a 6PPC early in the year. At the Mainville match Glenn put a .220 Russian barrel on the same rifle that had been a 6PPC earlier. He commented that while the .220 Russian was still a respectable shooter, tests had shown, and that weekend proved, it was a level below what he had gotten out of the PPC. Since it's tough enough to take home hardware that was the last time I saw the straight .220 Russian barrel. Ed Shilen tells us that one barrel doesn't prove anything. If you chambered up ten barrels, then shot them extensively, it might prove something. If that's the case you can see what the thousands of great shooting PPC barrels proves.

The 6PPC can give good results while shot in the higher pressure ranges. Some competitors like to use loads so hot they loosen primer pockets, and throw away the cases at the end of a days shooting. They reason that on a windy day the faster bullet will cut through the conditions better. (Let me warn any who try these firecracker loads, if you go to the oven often enough you'll eventually burn your finger, refer back to the chapter on safety). Jim Stekl and his 6BR attempted to use the 6mm bullet with a little more case capacity for higher velocity. Jim had good success with it in competition. I used one to shoot my first aggregate in the .1's. A .1936 Heavy Varmint Aggregate at 100 yards paved the way for a Three-Gun Aggregate victory in the IBS Nationals in 1981. In 1982 I had that 6BR barrel cut off, and rechambered for 6PPC. Complete record keeping paid dividends when inspection showed the rifle now averaged smaller groups, and aggregates. As a 6BR the smallest target ever fired from that barrel was a .118″ group @ 100 yards. As a 6PPC four months later it shot an .081″. The average grand aggregate shot in 1982 as a 6PPC dropped to .2885. That's a good way to fill up the walls of the trophy room. Consistency - and - small groups.

The new lot of SAKO brass with the 6PPC headstamp became available late in 1988. The initial run has less internal volume because of a thicker web area. Tests over the last few years have shown the 6PPC could be very slightly over volume for a 68 grain bullet, the new case might keep us from having to set barrels back if the theory proves out. Since it has less volume than old lot brass it creates tight cases if you try to shoot your old loads which were worked out with larger case volume.

Any shooter just getting into bench rest should be advised to stick with the 6PPC till they learn more and want to experiment. It borders on stupidity to knowingly get stuck with anything else as a first rifle. One of my greatest joys is taking someone at the public shooting range, who is wrestling with a Remington 700 BDL in 7 Mag, and let them shoot one of my PPC varmint rifles. They'll have proudly shown the best group ever shot with their rifle. Pasted to the shooting box top would be a ragged hole of around .485″ or maybe even .442″; the best group from ten or fifteen years of effort. I let them drop the firing pin on an empty chamber a few times so they don't accidently let one go (ever notice how even when you tell someone it's a two ounce trigger, they still blunder into it the first time a finger gets inside the guard). The two ounce trigger alone is enough to get a real shooter bouncing up and down a little. Then letting them shoot five shots downrange, as you watch the wind and coach when to touch the trigger. Eyes light up when the first two, then three, then all five are in one hole. The average, even from someone who has never fired a group in their life, is in the .3's. The very first group out of a real bench gun blows away the whole fifteen years pasted in that box top. From then on I have to shake them off since they want to go again and again. Solve that problem by always having a spare, used, 6PPC to sell the new shooter. You do the uninitiated a world of good by steering them away from something which won't work as well. I can relate to being taken for a ride by someone who was only interested in my checkbook. A joker traded me a Remington 788, 26″ Douglas barrel, stock trigger, wood stocked .222. He said: "Oh yea, this is competitive, just cut off the barrel, and put it into a fibreglass stock". Do benchrest a favor and become a guiding light on the right path. By the way, I never saw that clown again, this sport quickly weeds out the dishonest.

The PPC and its cousins are far and away the usual choice for todays benchrest shooters. The most common of the other options is the .222 Remington. The .222, designed by benchrest shooter Mike Walker, has been in top form since it's 1950 introduction. Originally developed as a

*Benchrest shooters always spend time discussing better ways to do things. John Jones and Henry Christman work on part of the puzzle while waiting for their relay.*

varmint cartridge for the "average shooter" the accuracy world soon found it to give groups as good or better than anything then available. Another benchrest shooter, Warren Page, along with Charlie Morse, finding phenomenal accuracy in field trials insisted that benchrest rifles be made for the caliber. With only two weeks of testing Mike Walker used one at the Nationals for second in the 100 yard Aggregate and second in the Grand Aggregate. Several shooters still use the .222 and its variations. Fast flying Larry Baggett of Levelland, Texas and action maker Allan Hall of Clanton, Alabama use .222 based rifles for most of their events.

The .219 Donaldson Wasp's first variant saw the light of day about 1933. Harvey Donaldson tested several styles before settling on a case formed from .219 Winchester Zipper brass. Harvey had produced a balanced case which achieved better accuracy with six grains less powder than the parent case. In the early years hundreds of shooters, using hundreds of rifles, all found the combination to be extremely accurate. The classic Wasp case used from 27 to 31 grains of 4320, and from 26 to 29 grains of 3031. The top loads are now recognized to be over the safe pressure limit. Muzzle velocity with a 55 grain bullet approached 3600 fps.

The 6mm American is a 1980's version of the Wasp. Several people, among them David Tooley, Nick Young, Jim Stekl, Harold Broughton, and Jim Schultz worked on the design. I saw Jim Stekl and Mike Walker several years ago shooting a case they called the American. They pulled a few strings and had some 30-30 Remington cases made up using a 22 Hornet primer pocket punch. They reformed these small rifle primer 30-30 cases (with a 22 Hornet base stamp) into a case with about PPC capacity. Dave Brennan spent two years bull dogging Federal Cartridge Corporation and Hugh Reed till they came up with some match quality brass. The new Federal 30-30 base case with a small primer hole (the headstamp has F C on the top and 30 AMERICAN around the bottom) could be reformed into many different wildcats. Tests were made on velocity from various length cases. The desired velocity of 3300 fps came with a case body length of 1.315″. An advantage of using this case for wildcat research is its rimmed design. Bolts for 30-30 are used, or it can be trimmed to fit the .308 and PPC bolt faces commonly found in benchrest rifles.

Since the .22 PPC seemed a little over bore, Dan Dowling of Arvada, Colorado created the 22 Waldog. A PPC base case is shortened .125″ to reduce the powder capacity and bring the cartridge into balance. Bill Pond of Rapid City, South Dakota used one in 1982 for a 100 yard aggregate below .1800. T322, H322, IMR 4198, BLC 1 for those who have hoarded it, and 748 are the most popular powders. 26 grains of powder and a 52 grain benchrest bullet give a velocity above 3350 on the chronograph.

Jim Stekl of Mohawk New York devised the .22BR and 6BR. They've shot well and won some matches, but early problems with case stickiness drove them deeply out of favor with competitive shooters. Remington redesigned the case, and finally released made to length brass in 1988. One criticism with American-made brass has always been its lack of concentricity. This new Remington brass was made with extra effort and attention paid to manufacturing super quality brass, only time will tell if the BR can shoot well enough to crawl out of the swamp in which it's languished.

For historical reference we'll mention the 6X47, the .222 Remington Magnum necked up to .243. First made in 1960 for Bob Hutton of GUNS AND AMMO Magazine, the case was used in the Sporter class where rules call for a bullet larger than .224″. The cartridge was a test bed for the early 6mm benchrest bullets: Clarence Detsch led the way in producing superb bullets for it. At the time Clarence was the only 6mm bullet maker selling hand made benchrest bullets: he sold those jewels to people who would use them for accuracy purposes. The 6X47 runs into pressure problems before developing enough velocity to really buck the wind. The 6PPC killed it deader than a mackerel.

The 6PPC performs well in so many rifles with so many bullets because all the different pieces work in harmony; the design could easily stand as the top dog for as long as the .222 Remington. My recommendation for anyone interested in shooting good groups and aggregates. Use the 6PPC in a good rifle and never be sorry.

# 5

# *Benchrest Bullets*

Benchrest quality bullets are made to very high tolerances: .0002″ is a big measurement in the life of a bullet. Rorschach (the premier bullet making die manufacturer) electric discharge machines the tungsten carbide core seater with a spindle which has less than .000025″ (twenty-five millionths of one inch) runout.

Early hand made benchrest bullets were made in two piece dies such as the ones available from RCBS. Fred Huntington of RCBS made available to the public a 90 grain .243 bullet around 1950. Bob Wallack commented at the time: "this .243 inch is so nearly a .25 caliber that it is hard for one to see any reason for it to be in existence". How times change.

Ray Biehler and Walt Astles developed the design ideas of Jonas Hallgrimsson. Jonas had done extensive testing of the available bullets, and in a search for something better, worked out the expanding-up process of making bullets. Expand-up is the process in use today. Early bullet making dies were made to final size. Because of the different expansion rates of jacket material and core material, when a core was pressed into jacket of final size there was often a small amount of expansion of the jacket leaving a loose core. The core was loose only a miniscule amount, but it was still a loose core. Biehler and Astles searched till they found a source of concentric jackets. They prepared a precise core swage, a special die seated the lead core firmly enough to expel all air and thoroughly fill the bottom of the jacket. The die was barely larger than the jacket and core, (.002″- .003″) it allowed the jacket and core to expand slightly, the inert lead core retains its upset size, when pressure is released the jacket wants to "spring back" to it's original dimension, end result was a perfect fit between core and jacket. The payoff was a bullet more perfect than anything then available, soon everyone had a set of B&A dies or shot bullets made in them (or were

*Another photo showing two major points. Nice guys can finish first, and you don't have to be young and mobile to shoot benchrest. The late Woody Cahall shows off the New Jersey Heavy Varmint Championship trophy.*

waiting on the back order list). In the early days of the expanding up process Sierra, then Hornady and Speer used it to produce bullets which rivaled the best home-made product. They had listened to the rumblings started by the accuracy nut - and the public was better off because of it.

One of the important factors in the number of competitive rifles on the line at any given match is the quality of the bullets available to all the competitors. In the old days, when a great lot of bullets were made they were closely guarded, and only shot in big matches or perfect days. The steel dies in use at the time would wear during use; they had a limited lifetime. Just because a set of dies would make a great bullet, at the 30,000 count it would have noticeably worn, and the product might begin to deteriorate. Tungsten Carbide dies with their life of millions and millions of bullets means investment in a quality set of dies will have them available for generations, not one or two years. (Tungsten Carbide dies which have made 2,500,000 bullets show less than one-tenthousandths of one inch of wear.)

Pick up a bullet and look at it. You'll note benchrest bullets have a hollow point, the hollow point design was chosen for target bullets to keep as much weight as possible at the maximum bullet diameter. The shooter who buys his bullets needs to measure and make a determination as to their potential accuracy. To measure a bullet you need a 1/10,000 inch micrometer. As you grade the first bullet something strange will become apparent. There's a small "ring" at the base of a flat base bullet which is .0002" to .0004" greater than the portion just forward of the base. The true bullet diameter is recognized as the portion just forward of the ring. Because of the small chance for out of roundness error in the custom bullet makers dies you only need to check a few out of each lot to ensure they're ok. It's generally acknowledged that bullets from groove diameter to .0003" under groove diameter will give acceptable results. Some tests have shown that groups open up when bullets are greater than .0002" above groove diameter. Like anything else in life there are exceptions.

The greatest fault that detracts from potential bullet accuracy is the concentricity of the jacket measurements. All other things being equal, THE QUALITY OF THE JACKETS DETERMINES THE QUALITY OF THE FINISHED BULLET. The bullet maker takes jacket wall measurements with a ball micrometer at several places around the circumference, usually at the base and at a point about half way between the base and the mouth. Variation of not greater than .0002"-.0003" is the goal for the really superb bullets we all want for perfect conditions, .0004"-.0005" jackets can be used at any of the windy shoots, and jackets with larger variations shouldn't be used in competition.

The faint grooves formed on the forward portion of the bullet (ogive wrinkles) have no effect on accuracy. One thing which does have significance is a "folded" jacket. This is where a weak spot in the mouth of the jacket collapsed in upon itself in a deep wrinkle. The bullet maker should have felt the difference in forming pressure, inspected, and discarded the error. Some bulletmakers product that I've shot has never had a folded jacket in the box, in anothers who's not as careful, I've found as many as two folded jackets per box. Shoot one of them at your record group and you'll be sorry!

Weigh some sample bullets from the new lot. If bullet weight is consistent to within two or three tenths of a grain there will be no noticeable difference in the targets. If the variation is greater than half a grain test some heavy ones and light ones at the shooting bench, if they impact at different points consider rejecting the lot. As with any benchrest bullet the final test is to shoot them. It's the only experiment that counts!

All bullets are not created equal. Any of the pills made by the custom makers are held to close tolerances, they're made with care and precision, (it commonly takes 11-12 hours to make 1000 bullets). It's the variations in diameter, length, ogive, bearing surface, and weight which gives us reason to experiment. Case neck walls need to be set for the bullet in use. Tight necks jammed into the chamber walls do nothing for accuracy (that's saying it politely). The powder charge and seating depth need adjusting between makers, and sometimes between lots from the same maker. The bullets in the box are as perfect as can be made. We have to discover the loading combination which allows them to sparkle.

The point where a bullet is at its most accurate is the combination that stabilizes the bullet quickly, as close to the muzzle as possible. The bullet length, diameter, and muzzle velocity helps calculate the rate of twist which stabilizes the bullet best. According to Paul J. Hart of Hart Rifle Barrels the slowest twist which stabilizes the bullet will be the most accurate. Dr. Franklin Mann tested stabilization by firing a bullet through a series of screens placed between the firing line and the butt. He found bullets weren't always perfectly stable, sometimes they go into and out of stable flight. In benchrest rifles most bullets exhibit some yaw early in their flight, before "going to sleep". The less yaw the better, it's the complete lack of yaw which makes the "hummer" barrel shoot through conditions better. The quicker a bullet stabilizes the less effect wind will have on its flight.

# 6

# *The Bench and Bench Technique*

No matter how accurate the rifle, without a steady bench and rests groups will be poor. Just as a rifleman standing on his own two legs tries to control movement, the benchrest shooter must maintain perfect sight alignment during trigger squeeze, and follow through. For this reason the steadier the bench, the better the shooting. Anyone that's been around has seen some crazy shooting benches, and rests. There are the movable benches on multi purpose ranges with rounded corners from being dragged across the pavement to put them into position. Shooting off one of them is like dating a belly dancer, you know what you want to do but the target keeps moving through your sight picture. There are the folded up jackets, hats, and gun cases on the car's front hood while trying to sight in Uncle Charlie's hunting rifle. My favorites are the home made jobs people bring in the back of their car, they weigh so much it takes a gorilla to get them out of the trunk. We have enough limiting factors in shooting a good group, let's not make it any tougher. Set up a good solid bench, and rests, before anything else.

The current style bench has evolved since the turn of the century into its present form. From the legs up the bench must be steady. The legs can be 3″ or 4″ pipe filled with cement, set into a ready mix filled hole dug to below the frost level, or filled cinder block on a poured concrete pad. Remember, the more permanent the better. Use whatever free construction help that's available, every club has someone who knows what materials are required for the local weather conditions.

The most durable and most comfortable top is made with four inches of concrete poured into a stubby "T" shaped form. The bench top needs to be big enough to hold all the tools, accessories, and ammo you'll use during

*Many benchrest shooters like to experiment with rifles and rests. Wilbur Cooper built this rifle and rest from scratch. This long "T" shaped bench has plenty of room.*

your shooting, skimping platform size leads to distractions down the road. Since the concrete form only makes one top at a time it's convenient to spread the construction of tops over a longer period. That way a few minutes every time the range is used soon produces a whole string of bench tops. Be sure to smooth the concrete surface. Nothing takes skin off the elbows faster than rough concrete during recoil. Wood tops were the norm for decades. Their tendency to warp over the years, even when sealed and covered by a roof, gives the adjustable pedestal rest a good workout as you move down the line. A top set to a height of 32" will suit most shooters. Those who need extra height on their stool should use one of the adjustables with a cushion. Anyone too tall for a 32" top is used to bending over, but is still comfortable. At your local range, everyone on the line will desire the use of that solid bench once it's constructed. If you don't want to get to the range at 5:00 AM every Sunday make more than one. Finish the bench off with a stool or chair. The adjustable stools as made by several PRECISION SHOOTING advertisers are the real ticket if you travel to matches and shoot at different ranges. Even on the same range the stool gets adjusted up and down because of slightly different bench heights and target angles. Tony Hidalgo and John Brown made the two I use. The only change was to nail carpeting to the top for more friction, after ten years and forty thousand rounds neither shows any wear. The rear is softer than plywood!

*The 13 pound Hart rest is one of the most popular among the benchrest shooters. Steady, but adjustable rests help anyone shoot better groups.*

Now that the bench is good and solid we need the pedestal, front sandbag, and rear sandbag to be sturdy enough to hold the rifle steady during loading, unloading, and sighting. Many people sight in their hunting rifle on a hard metal ammo box before deer season, then wonder why they miss a deer at 100 yards on opening day. Don't shoot off any hard object, or allow the rifle to be touching something hard during the shot. Even if you're in a tower deer stand, or a plywood shooting house, use some padding underneath the forend for rested shots. A rifle rest must approximate the recoil dampening tendencies of the hand and shoulder. Benchrest shooters have found the best accuracy comes from sand filled leather bags. The bags and pedestal must be adjustable when we want to set up, but they need to be steady when the shot is fired. For a front rest I like using the green cast pedestal rest Wally Hart of Robert W. Hart and Son sells. It's easily adjusted, very strong, durable, and available with several tops depending on your preference. I put a Wendell Coye Competition Top on it for Heavy Varmint, leave the standard top on for my CPS, aluminum stocked, Light Varmint. Some shooters use the black cast rest from Wichita, those who travel top drawer will get the crank adjustable rest from Bill Gebhardt of Bald Eagle. A top of the line rest is in the $90 - $130 range, but it will last for generations. The rest you should avoid is the orange Hoppe's rest. For top level benchrest accuracy it's not stable, or adjustable enough.

For a right hander it's the left hand that controls movement of the rear sandbag. By carefully sliding, squeezing, or flattening the bag the crosshairs move the amounts needed for initial and final aim. Advances have been made in sandbag design recently. Shooters at the turn of the century shot off wooden blocks, in the 1940's they used cloth bags filled with sand. Many of them rested the barrel on their front sandbag. Though you still see it at the public range, that tendency was gone from competitive benchrest by the 1950's. Experimentation had proven the barrel needed to vibrate under the same conditions on each shot. This meant free floating the barrel, or a good barrel bedding job by someone who knew what they were doing.

We now use smooth firm sandbags that conform to the shape of the forend and buttstock. The Protektor front and rear bags have been the favorites for years. Fitted front bags are made for each type of rifle. From "U" shaped bags that will fit any hunting rifle, to specific flat bottomed "U" shaped bags wide enough, and with a snug fit, for the two and a quarter inch hunter class forend, and three inch wide varmint class forend. The rear bag comes in two main configurations. A tapered four inch by six inch bag with low "Bunny Ears" (also called "Owl Ears") or with high "Rabbit Ears". After shooting extensively with both I chose the short ears. They don't interfere with my hand under recoil and provide more consistent friction shot to shot. On my aluminum stocked rifle I cut the friction even more by reversing that rear bag and resting the butt on only 1″ of leather. You'll find the cheap suede and vinyl bags don't work well, and wear out quickly. On the newest type of front bag, the competition top, screw levers on the front rest side plates adjust tension so the forend achieves an extra snug fit with little lateral play. With any of these setups the rifle can be returned to battery easily and quickly with only small adjustments needed to achieve perfect aim. Look at the accompanying photos and note the differences with what you may be using now. Experimentation is the lifeblood of benchrest. You'll soon find what's most comfortable for your particular style.

### Bench Technique

Bench technique is one area where the lines are hazy between absolute right and wrong. Each shooter should find a style that fits their body shape and personality. Just like the load for the rifle, the important thing is consistency. There are several points which have been proven as assets. Set up the bags pointed straight at the target. Apply baby powder or talcum to taste. Adjust the bags so the rifle will be supported at the same points for every shot. Lots of rifles have a piece of tape on the forend to indicate front rest placement. Gently tap down the bags to compact the sand. Adjust the front pedestal's star ring and the rear bag to get the crosshairs in the center

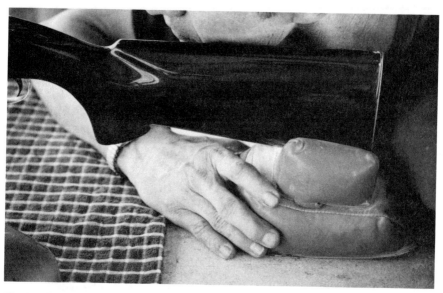

*Jim Williams shows off his technique for small groups. His right hand grips the rear sandbag for aim adjustment, his shoulder and cheek barely caress the stock.*

of the target. Check the recoil movement by pushing the rifle forward and back a few times. When the rifle is in the position of full recoil look through the scope and ensure it's not moved over to where the crosshairs are on your neighbors target. Realign the bags if the crosshairs move too far laterally on recoil. It's trouble if the rifle recoils onto someone else's target and you don't notice before letting go another shot. (Now who would do that?) It's easy to do when the targets are grouped close together like at some of the Gulf Coast shoots.

Set up your loaded rounds, ammo block, stop watch, and bolt in a convenient position; accessible placement is everything for fast shooting technique. The ammo is on the side of the loading port. You need a way to keep track of the number of shots in the record target. I deposit five rounds on a towel placed just below the loading port. These are my designated record rounds, any sighter shots will come out of the box. Since I freely shoot a record case at the sighter if the conditions change, I need a method to tell how many shots remain to finish the target. Before any record case is fired as a sighter another round is pulled from the MTM box and placed on the towel. Using this method I've never failed to fire all the record shots in several hundred matches. A bonus with the cases being on a towel is; it's very fast. You don't have to fiddle with placing an empty back in a block hole, just throw them down. (Ralph Council and Clyde Honea: "If the brass ain't flying you're dying"). Once in a while this means picking up cases off

*Portable shooting benches are wonderful for the long-range varmint hunter and the shooter who can't construct a permanent bench. Here's a popular design from Armor Metal Products.*

the ground, but they're none the worse for the brief, wild, ride. Other options include the one used by Jack Sutton. He places a case in the top of his opened MTM box after the shot goes into the record target. If there are only four cases in the box top he needs to launch another down range. Five shot groups are easier to keep track of, but ten shot heavy bench matches can get confusing after lots of sighter shots. Gary Ocock mentally counts each record shot, repeating the number over and over while waiting for the next shot. This causes some people trouble. Gary admits five shots are no problem; ten shot groups with their 12 minute time span can get tricky. Some people like Lester Bruno are so picky about the segregation of record and sighter cases they pull a record case from the chamber and insert a sighter case instead. If any of you have been to the Super Shoot we all saw Lester, on more than one occasion, have to borrow the next shooters rifle when the bullet pulled out of the case and powder went tumbling into the crevices of his single shot action. It's a credit to Lester's ability he finished those groups out, in the time limit, one of them with a .22 going into those 6mm holes. I like to stand behind the relay before mine and watch through a spotting scope. While I'm there to learn the days conditions it happens every weekend, someone exclaiming they don't remember how many record shots are in the target. Whenever they decide to shoot another - it will be their sixth - it will spoil the group. There are many options, ask what your friends use, experiment, find something consistent and comfortable.

Sit down to the bench at a 45 degree angle with both feet flat on the ground, relax and get comfortable. Some shooters like to have contact between the bench and ribs. If the bench is sturdy this doesn't detract from scope alignment. When the bench is wiggly, it can transmit heartbeats and muscle movement through to the rifle. With a very long torso I'm more comfortable with no contact or minimum contact. Use an adjustable stool and get your body in the same position for every group, no matter what the bench height. Without an adjustable stool if the top's too high you're upright, pulled away from the scope, and straining to reload. If the top's too low you're hunched over, presenting your eyebrow to the scope for a little kiss. Especially if you hold onto the rifle either of these change the shoulder angle to the buttstock and effect recoil tendencies.

There's a wide range of positions the shooter can use to hold the rifle. From no hold, free recoil, where the only part of the shooter touching the rifle is the trigger finger. To a hard hold with the hand, cheek and shoulder making heavy contact. There are many in betweens and that's where most competitive shooters settle, something short of a hard hold. Free recoil is the technique I settled on early in my first year of competition. I touch the trigger guard with my middle finger, it acts as a guide so I don't blunder into the trigger accidently, and the index finger is on the trigger. Another option for free recoil is to place the thumb behind the trigger guard. The finger as a guide becomes very important when the adrenaline rush comes into play during a tiny group. Watching Ed Watson when he's on a roll I don't see how he keeps shooting tiny groups while shaking from so much excitement.

I settle the rifle completely into tightly packed bags. Adjust the aim left or right with bag movement, elevation with the front rest screw. At any time I don't like more than a tiny amount of hand held rear bag deflection when the shot goes off. Many benchrest shooters squeeze the bag to adjust the aim on a shot. Then, if they unconsciously relax their hand just as the shot goes off, they get a flyer. How many of us have heard: "The first four were in the zeroes and the fifth one made it half an inch". Think specifically about this item next time you shoot; it's one of the common reasons for an extended slump.

Using the free recoil technique, if forced to, I'm able to get off five aimed shots in thirty seconds. That thirty seconds includes five shots and four reloads, almost eight seconds to reload and aim, plenty of time; however, as Don Geraci will tell you it's better to take just a little more time and be extra fine on the aim, tiny groups come from settling the cross hairs exactly before pulling the trigger.

There are lots of shooters who like to have a hold on their rifle during a group. They think it's easier to adjust the aim back into place quickly. With the option of different amounts of hand, shoulder and cheek pressure the key is to pick something that's comfortable and repeatable. My biggest

*Gary Vincent shoots bunches of tiny groups using a fast shooting style. Showing proper form he works on another successful outing.*

complaint with holding on to a rifle is the effect of muzzle blast from the shooter next door. Unconsciously we all flinch when the crack from next door hits us. As hero's, we don't like to admit it, but I'd bet nine out of ten people who complain their group was enlarged because they "doubled" were really the victim of a small flinch. Some claim the rifle's crosshairs move when shots around them go off. If it's happening at a range where you have the preferred six feet between centers on the benches, the bench, rests and rifle aren't settled properly. Try a firmer sand, or gravel and sand, filled bag. Read the rule book, no lead shot allowed. I cut down the chance for a flinch by wearing both ear plugs and ear muffs. Outside ranges without a roof aren't much of a problem, but metal range roofs reflect back a lot of noise. The second protective barrier significantly reduces noise flinching. You'll achieve better concentration, and consistently shoot better using both sets of ear protection.

Control of the competition two ounce trigger is something every benchrest shooter must practice and master. Even though it lets off easily and quickly the trained finger squeezes it just like the three pounder on a hunting rifle. With practice you'll use a graduated pull during days with better conditions. You can go through three or four distinct trigger finger pressure increases before the pin falls. Even though a benchrest rifle weighs at least ten and a half pounds, and is set solidly in sandbags, the aim can be disturbed if the trigger is yanked. Practice dry firing with an empty

*Jim Williams uses a flat sandbag to support his trigger hand and get better control of a 2 oz. trigger.*

chamber. The best trigger pull for a beginning shooter is similar to that used for a hunting rifle. Get the crosshairs aligned exactly on the aiming spot. Gradually, but quickly, increase finger pressure till the shot is fired. Look through the scope as the firing pin falls on the empty chamber. If the crosshairs don't move you have a deft enough touch for a two ounce.

At the same time this is a perfect opportunity to make sure there's no flinch. Even though bench rifles in their small calibers only produce four foot pounds of recoil many shooters flinch slightly. This could be caused by bad experiences with big, booming, hurting, magnum, hunting rifles. Some people are noise sensitive. Whatever the reason, test to make sure you're not flinching. First, and most important, make up your mind you're not going to flinch. Get a buddy to alternately load a round, or leave an empty chamber while you're turned around and not looking. Since you don't know if the gun will fire, when the pin falls on an empty chamber it will show if you're jerking the trigger, or flinching, and moving the crosshairs. When you've gone into a slump, run some dry fire practice and see if it's a flinch, or trigger yank which has caused the trouble.

Breath control is not nearly so important in benchrest as in the other rifle sports. Where a free rifleman must be certain to watch breathing patterns as his sight picture wanders, with our steady rests, benchrest shooters can give it some leeway. Being able to avoid worrying about breath control is one of the reasons I shoot free recoil. The breathing cycle contains a normal, slight, pause at the end of exhalation. We would like to increase the pause and release the shot in the next five or ten seconds. Get into a rhythm with your breathing and it soon becomes second nature to fire the shot at the proper moment.

One item Bob White and I liked to discuss was how to set up for our sighter shots. With a sloping buttstock there are three ways to do it. First is to leave the forend in the same position and slide the rear bag backward to lower the muzzle to the sighter target. Second is to leave the bags in the same place and slide the rifle forward for the same effect. Third is to adjust the height of the front or rear rest with screw adjustment. I've always been most comfortable sliding the rear bag. It's quick, the rifle is still supported close to it's center of gravity, and the return to the record target is easily accomplished. Bob liked to move the whole rifle. He thought my way caused flyers while moving back up to the record target. I say the same thing about his way. By leaving the front support, the one closer to the center of gravity, consistent I feel better about my rifles accuracy. The third is used mostly with heavy bench guns and their flat butt stocks. It would support the Varmint rifle in exactly the same way for record and sighter shots but without cams it's much too slow for match shooting.

# 7

# *What is a Match*

Benchrest matches are wondrous events. There are widgets, gadgets, moans, groans, chuckles, laughs, exultation, and consternation. In short, a benchrest match is a slice of life. The many participants who make up a competitive field bring all walks of life to the arena. This conglomeration gets along better than any group I've ever seen. Weekends spent in the company of benchrest shooters are always interesting, lifelong friends, and newcomers will all participate in a rewarding exercise.

The entire family is welcome at any benchrest match, many shooters include the youngsters in their travel plans. A pop-up trailer, or big tent, will house the clan cheaply and conveniently. Travelling to a far away match with your group can combine a little vacation and a shoot all in one. Some of the big matches have gained a reputation as family events. The Crawfish Invitational in Lafayette, Louisiana runs an advertised program for the wives who don't shoot. They tour old houses, shop, eat out, and bone up on local history. Then, after a days sightseeing, the group comes back to the range for a crawfish boil. 800 pounds of crawfish, buckets of potatoes, corn, and hot sauce disappear in an instant. Another match that's fun to attend is the Cactus Classic, held north of Phoenix, Arizona. The first week of March is a good time to leave the snow and icicles of the north country and head down for some sun. As the first big match of the year the Cactus gathers some tough shooters together for an early challenge. In 1989 the Cactus decided to throw down the gauntlet and punish any of the 161 shooters who weren't prepared. The Friday before the match there was a big rainstorm complete with hail, Saturday the cold North winds whistled through the range, anyone expecting to work on their sun tan was in for a rude awakening. On Friday, Gary Ocock got together with the Pennsylvania crowd he had left behind when he moved to Phoenix, they decided on some

*When we say that benchrest matches are family affairs we mean it! Rip Novak sports the latest in gun dog apparel at a match.*

impromptu mountain climbing. Only problem was, Gary fell off a big rock and banged up his foot (there's still some dispute about whether Gary fell, or if he was pushed). Unlike the ankle, his shooting skill was none the worse for the wear, while on crutches he clobbered the rest of us in the two gun.

Several people schedule their whole vacation around which matches they plan to attend. The big three are: the Super Shoot - a four day event over the Memorial Day weekend held at Kelbly's Ohio range, the NBRSA Nationals - a week long event the end of July, and the IBS Nationals - a long weekend the end of August. A few people I've seen a long way from home include Ira Farnsworth of New Hampshire and H. J Fedorowich from London, Canada. The long distance driving champs the last several years must be Dennis Wagner of Bethany, Oklahoma and Lowell Frei of St. George, Utah. They've driven for long distances to participate in both large and small events. For Dennis, the Midland, Texas range is his second closest match, you know there's a lot of driving involved. Several people like Bob DeMonstoy, George Kelbly, and Paul J. Hart plan a swing which includes several matches. A good choice, depending on how much time you have, is to hit the Cactus the first week-end in March, then to Lafayette the next week-end for the Crawfish warm-up, sight- see for a couple of weeks, shoot the Crawfish, then go home and get ready for the Super Shoot.

*Travelling companions increase the enjoyment of a match. Someone to chat with passes the time on the road; it's usually a friendly rivalry during the match.*

Dave Brennan and PRECISION SHOOTING Magazine increased the airline traffic by creating the Benchrest Shooter Of The Year award. Points for this award can be won at several matches. They include the big three, plus a few local matches from each organization. In 1987 the early match here in Tomball, Texas was a designated match. Hall of Fame member Perry Morton flew all the way down from Warsaw, Indiana to shoot, and try for points. That wasn't his best weekend, but he achieved enough points at his other matches to be named for the award. Perry, among other titles, was the NBRSA National Champion in Light Varmint, and the Two Gun, he was the IBS National Champion in Light Varmint, and the Three Gun. To the victor go the spoils. In this case, you get your picture on the cover of PRECISION SHOOTING, and at the next years Super Shoot your friends give you a formal roasting. (To watch one of these roasts is worth the trip to the Super Shoot.)

## Step by Step Instructions for Your First Match

First item of business is packing up the equipment required to shoot the event. During a winter league match you might be pre loaded (if you're smart, and the loading area is outside - that is.) Then, all that's required are rifle, rests, loaded ammo, hearing protectors, warm clothes, and a few bucks for the entry fee. When it's a registered match, fired over two days, the list expands to include loading tools, components and measures. Nothing's so frustrating as driving several hours to a registered match and leaving a loading box, bolt, or cases sitting in the middle of the garage. Headed for Camillus my first year I forgot a loading box, it's not fun. Then again, the rifle you borrow might be more accurate than your own.

The next item is one of the most important; you have to find the place. A rifle range is just like a race track. Since it's noisy a range isn't right in the middle of town where it's easy to find. Ask Geza Nagy about spending a whole night, driving round and round some mountain in the middle of Canada, trying to find a range. If you have time to send a letter, ask for a map from the host club. The best way to find a range is by travelling with another shooter who knows where it is. This kills two birds with one stone: a companion fills the time spent on the road, they're also a sounding board for the hundreds of questions about benchrest that fill your brain. Bob White has suffered through thousands of questions (and statements) over the hundreds of hours we've spent driving to matches. Those hundreds of hours are filled with some unbelievable events. My very first match was January 10, 1981. A winter league shoot in Englishtown, New Jersey the thermometer was at 10 degrees Fahrenheit. With a north wind howling across the exposed firing line, and loading area, who knows what the wind chill was. Bob White, Fred Finlay, and I drove down in Bob's VW camper van. The heater didn't work. Shaking from head to toe the groups I shot at 100 yards ranged from .660″ to 1.865″. That sounds more like a 300 yard aggregate (and a bad one at that). Driving the day before the 1982 IBS Nationals at Kelbly's, Bob and I had the shock absorber punch a hole through the VW's oil filter. When the oil spread itself over the Western Pennsylvania countryside the engine decided to stop in a hurry. Getting the van to a service station six hours from home we found the only place to rent cars was a regional airport an hour east, back down Route 80. We finally arrived at the range 4:00 in the morning. Doc Maretzo had been telling everyone: "I don't know where they are, I passed them on the highway"; ten shot groups in Heavy Bench weren't fun that morning. Another time coming back from Painted Post the front caliper bolts worked their way out. We couldn't drive that way because of a bad shudder, after trying a few things I got the bright idea of pounding a 6BR case into the caliper bolt hole. It was a nice force fit and we were on the road again, (see, the BR is good for something). Problem was, applying the brakes crossing the Delaware River Bridge forced the BR case out. After removing the wheel again, and fitting another, we drove the next hour without touching the brakes. The hills of Chester were kind of exciting that night. Fred Finlay, driving the van home to work on it, had it catch fire and burn to the ground a short while later. Fred said it was kind of exciting for a few minutes there. With the sound of the fire crackling in his ears he was trying to pull out some of the cargo. Included were a couple of benchrest rifles and some other

*The bench set-up of Charlie Mills. Everything is easily accessible for fast shooting.*

boxes. He had placed a canvas hunting jacket over his head while he removed the items. Another passer by tapped Fred on the back and said: "By the way you're on fire". I saw the site of the funeral pyre a few weeks later, pieces of engine were melted into the pavement. It was about time for that camper to go off to VW heaven; I had decided to never travel in it again.

Once you've found the range the rest of the weekend is downright delightful. For a two day match it's easy to camp at the range. That's what I like to do. By not having to pay for a hotel room it cuts the weekend's expenses 50% or more. Depending on the distance I can get a two day match for $75.00 - $100.00, including entry fee, if I'm frugal. Camping at the range gives a chance to get in the spirit right from the first night. If you've had to work that Friday before traveling to the match it will probably be dark when you arrive. Ask directions to the firing line and go out and wander among the wind flags. It's an eery feeling, wandering among the flags. They're already spinning, squeaking, rattling, and trying to tell you the conditions. The only ranges where I don't go out and bump into the night are the ones with rattlesnakes.

If you spent the night at a hotel plan on getting to the range plenty early. If you're in a van, or tent, roll out, grab a shooter, ask them where to sign up. If it's a registered match you need to be a member of IBS or NBRSA. If you're not a member yet sign up at the match, the people in the range shack are more than helpful. Taking the equipment card they hand you fill in the spaces. It asks for your name, address (so you get a match report) what class you're firing in, what caliber, barrel maker, gunsmith, scope, magnification, and a few other simple questions. The statistician will assign a relay, bench, and competitor number for the match. The competitor number will stay the same for the whole weekend, it will be on every target you fire at (of course, one time at Mainville Jack Deming shot on my target, maybe he didn't like the one he had). Let's say this match is the early Mainville shoot. The two events will be Heavy Varmint in the morning, Light Varmint in the afternoon. Someone was wise enough to set you up with a 10 1/2 pound 6PPC so the same rifle can be used in both classes. You got lucky and were assigned competitor 116. The number combines your relay and bench number into one. The first one means relay one, the 16 means bench 16 on the first relay. If it was 216 that would be relay two, bench 16.

At this first match you're sure to be excited, and nervous. Apply the fundamentals you've learned in practice, strive to do your best. Since you're on the first relay, the range shack will have told you the first relay starting time. Usually this is around eight o'clock. Get all your shooting gear ready, set up the loading tools for later, patch out the rifle, double check the ammo, saunter over to bench 16 with your rests. Depending on the range you might be able to set up your rests with the rifle in position. This means with the bolt out. Benchrest rifles **always** have their bolts out until the commence fire command. Safety is paramount since the range crew might be placing targets and backers downrange. Most competitors stuff their bolt into a bolt holster. A few don't, sticking it in a pocket, or leaving it on the loading block, they're usually the ones sprinting back to their loading table when the range officer says commence fire.

Get to the bench plenty early. Set up, introduce yourself to the shooters on each side, they'll be there for the rest of the weekend. For this first match it's best to come with a rifle that's already sighted in. Nothing's more frustrating than problems sighting in a rifle during the first match. You need concentration for the task at hand not on hitting a piece of paper in a time limit. Different ranges run their first warm-up or sight in match different, depending on the number of shooters and relays. I like the warm-up to be a full match. It may have been a while since this load and rifle have been fired, the early morning temperature will probably be lower than last time you shot. The warm-up is used to experiment with the days conditions, something you can't do if the shots count. Most of the NBRSA ranges run a three minute sight in period in front of the record match, rather than a full warm-up match. This works unless someone who has changed barrels or scopes has problems and shoots all their loaded ammo before getting on paper. Then we all wait till they load up some more. Find out what type of warm-up will be used and be ready.

Since you're sighted in the warm-up match is a piece of cake. The very best conditions of the day allow a nice confidence builder for the first group.

*The score sheet always attracts a crowd when it's updated with each relays results. "Look at that - my .143" was small group of the second match."*

Other than time considerations here's the only thing wrong with a full warm-up match. If you shoot a barn burner it won't count in the record string. Most ranges will have scales with certified weights set up. Before or after the warm-up the range officer will call all the competitors on the relay to the scale for weigh-in. This is where you find out if the rifle really does weigh the correct amount. If you've got a 10 1/2 pounder the morning weigh-in and its 13 1/2 pound limit is no problem, the rifle will probably still make weight even with a box of shells on the scale.

The Range Aggregate consists of five record groups shot consecutively with one class of rifle. The five record groups shot on your first morning would be a 100 yard Heavy Varmint Range Aggregate. At Mainville the afternoon event would be the 100 yard stage for 10 1/2 pound rifles. Here's another beauty of firing one rifle in both classes. The rifle and load are perfectly worked out after the mornings competition. The days wind and mirage effect on the rifle and load are familiar. It's easy to be consistent since nothings changed. At the end of the day we will have fired two 100 yard aggregates. Then begins one of the best times of the match. After cleaning up it's easy to find someone for dinner if you want to go out. I like to stay at the range with a steak on the barbecue. Then I can walk around to all the different groups and spend the evening wandering into and out of various conversations. Bob White, Jim Novak and I had a favorite sport at the Mainville and Council Cup matches. We broke out a Bocce Ball set and played into the night. It never mattered who won, we consumed some of Mr Busch's finest, busted each other's chops, and had a good time in general. The socialization is as important as the match itself in comparison of enjoyment levels.

The next morning, it's up at 6:00, start loading the cases for the first match. I wake up stiff in the morning, those around me take bets to see which letter my body has been formed into overnight. Lots of ranges have kitchen's open for breakfast. The only time I **ever** eat eggs is at a rifle range. There must be some unwritten law we have to be served eggs at a match. By 7:30 it's time to move your rests to the line and get ready for the 200 yard stage of Heavy Varmint. The competitor number and first bench will be the same as yesterday: bench sixteen, relay one.

Shooting at the 100 yard range I like my point of impact from a center hold to be on the bottom edge of the bull. This keeps the aiming spot from being shot out. If we were to hit exact point of aim at 100 yards we would lose our aiming point, and ability to hold fine, after the bullets cut out the ring. At 200 yards the bull is large enough this isn't an issue. It's best to try for an impact in, or touching the bull. Chasing shots is much easier at the longer yardages with a center point of impact (you'll also like a center point of impact for when you show good groups to your buddies). With a PPC put six clicks of vertical into a Leupold 36X scope to compensate for 200 yards and the day's off to a good start. During the warm-up or sight-in you should only need one or two clicks left or right depending on how hard the wind was blowing yesterday. It's easy to have problems getting on paper at 200 yards if you've changed the rifle, barrel, or scope since yesterday. When that's the case it's best to sight in the new combination the night before during free shooting time. To repeat: it's important to get the point of impact close to the bull. Later in the day, when the wind and mirage come into play, trouble looms if your impact is already on the downwind side.

Today is an exact repeat of yesterday, except it's at 200 yards. The bench rotation is the same, the competitors next to you are the same. The five groups are now called the Heavy Varmint 200 yard aggregate. The 200 yard aggregate gets averaged with the 100 yard aggregate to make a Grand Aggregate. When the 200 yard stage for the second rifle is finished, averaged with the 100 yard stage for a grand aggregate, and added to the Heavy Varmint Grand Aggregate it becomes a Two Gun Aggregate. NBRSA uses a slightly different format. They shoot the 100 and 200 yard aggregates for one class on the same day. Usually Light Varmint is fired the first day, Heavy Varmint comes the second day.

Whichever path is used to reach it, the Two-Gun Aggregate is the whole ball of wax. When you win it you're the most complete shooter at the match. Some other competitor probably beat you in one, or two, or all of the individual range aggregates. The multi gun aggregate shows true rifle accuracy and shooter competence. Consistency during the individual groups and aggregates is always rewarded with high placings. A good way to tell when you're starting to shoot well is when you make Marge Masker's list. Marge calculates scores, and keeps track of quite a few people during the match. She'll always be able to tell you: how Seely and Jerry are doing, who's in the lead, who's closing in, and who just threw away their chances. Read the chapter on practice and competition to start moving up the standings toward an aggregate victory.

# 8

# *Wind Shooting*

The most important thing to remember in group shooting is: any wind, from any direction, pushes the bullet during its flight. This lesson is to bring home the importance of this. We have all heard the unknowing say: "But that bullet is travelling too fast to be pushed by the wind" - wrong! Wind moves a supersonic airplane, wind pushes a blasting off moon rocket, wind effects a 250 pound linebacker running down field. The truth is that a lighter bullet moving slower is pushed farther than a heavier bullet moving faster, but they all move!

Let's clear up a few fundamentals.

1. The rifle must be reasonably accurate; however, the most inaccurate of rifles can be helped by wind sense.
2. The loaded round should be the best worked out for that rifle, this typically means handloads.
3. Get proper targets.
   A. For low power scopes the IBS or NBRSA Hunter target is best. It's easy to repeat aim and hold off with the center circle on this type of target.
   B. For high power scopes (16x-36x) use the standard benchrest target. For the finest in accuracy the resolution a high magnification scope is necessary to precisely change point of aim. With a 36X scope it's possible to aim at the left or the right side of a bullet hole at 100 yards.
4. Refer to the chapter on solid bench construction. Any movement from a wiggly bench gives larger groups

## Wind Effect

There are many general indicators of what the wind is doing. What we feel on our body, what we see by the movement of objects around us, and where sighter shots impact compared to the winds angle and intensity.

Since judgement of the wind is so important in shooting a small group it's time to build a few wind flags. These can be simple, such as a drilled piece of 5/8″ dowel, with a piece of surveyors tape on a bent coat hanger, inserted into a drilled hole. Six simple flags can be made in 15 minutes and they're all you need to get started. Early on spend your time at the range shooting groups, not in the workshop building flags.

Wind deflection of the bullet is a matter of weighted averages.

1. Direct crosswinds from 3:00 and 9:00 will have more effect than angled winds from closer to 12:00 and 6:00.
2. The closer the wind movement is to the muzzle the more effect it will have on final impact point. Bullets have some amount of yaw when they leave the muzzle. Any wind deflection has a greater effect on the bullet before it stabilizes.
3. Wind has its greatest effect when the bullet is at its highest rate of velocity loss. (Close to the muzzle.)

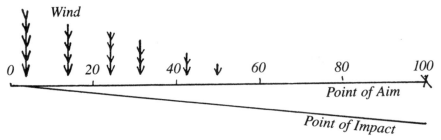

This heavy push close to the muzzle will deflect much more than an identical heavy push at the target. The simplified reason for this is.

1. When the angle of flight is changed early the bullet spends more time on an angle that's no longer straight at the bulls eye - it's moving out of the group.
2. A bullet deflected later in its flight should already be stabilized, the wind doesn't have as much effect as earlier in the flight. The bullet doesn't spend as much time on this new angle and impacts closer to point of aim. Of course, reading the wind gets tricky when the front and back half are each doing something different. To achieve your best groups in the beginning try to shoot when the flags all show the same wind direction and intensity. Even as you gain experience steady conditions are the best group producers.

Let's shoot a sample target and see how the wind influences each shot. For example purposes we have a breeze from exactly 9:00 and the only variation is intensity.

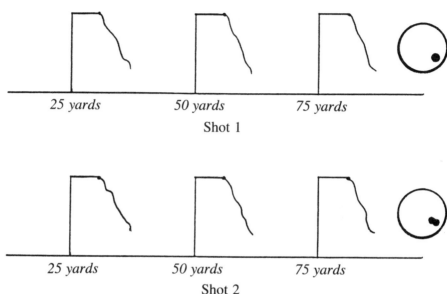

Shot 1

Shot 2

In the same condition shot number two hits shot number one.

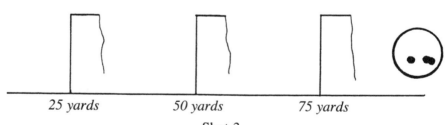

Shot 3

Reading the flags you can see the decrease in velocity has dropped the shot to the left.

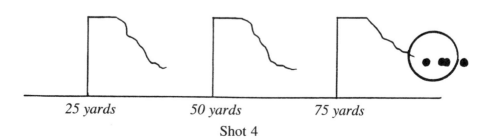

Shot 4

This time an increase at 50 and 75 yards has pushed our bullet to the right.

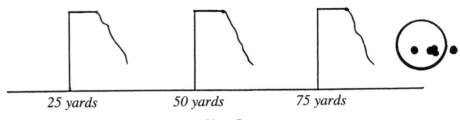

|  25 yards  |  50 yards  |  75 yards  |

Shot 5

When the same wind velocity as shots one and two returns we put number five very close to the group.

In our example both misses can now be explained. At the local range I've witnessed the spoiling of many good groups by non wind conscious shooters. They would fire two times in a hard blow left to right, then have the wind back around to hard right to left, and wonder why the third shot was so far out of the group.

In the early 1900's C.W. Rowland spent as much as two days shooting a group: he waited for calm conditions before triggering a shot. In competition we don't have unlimited time to wait for the perfect condition to return. That's when the sighter target is invaluable. The record (top) portion of the target must end up with five shots in it; the bottom portion is for sighters, and can be shot at an unlimited number of times during the match.

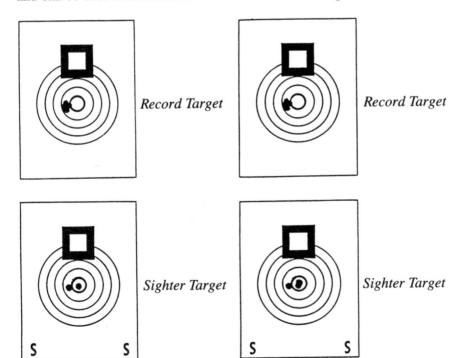

*Record Target*

*Record Target*

*Sighter Target*

*Sighter Target*

In a calm condition, one shot was fired at the sighter to check impact, it struck the center of the aiming circle. The wind increased to a gentle right to left breeze that looked like it will hold steady. With the same hold the first four record shots were fired under these stable conditions. They grouped into a nice .220″ group. The initial calm settled in before the fifth shot could be fired. Running out of time the sighter must be used to put number five into the group. Moving the crosshairs to the sighter portion a shot was loosed, it impacted with the first calm condition sighter. To put the record shot in the group, observe the amount of bullet deflection and hold the same distance to the left. By aiming for this new location number five landed in the middle of the first four shots. In our example this would be a dead on hold in the center of the group.

Congratulations, the small group was preserved. Without holding off we would have blown this one to half an inch.

### Let's Review the Basics

1. Wind moves the bullet depending upon direction and intensity. Physics dictate that wind moves a bullet regardless of initial velocity
2. Wind flags show the wind velocity and direction. Without flags you have no idea whether another shot will impact with the last.
3. Believe in the benchrest rifle. If a shot is out - look down range and find the flags that explain the bullet deflection.
4. Use the sighter portion of the target to show where a particular condition makes a shot print. Factor in visible wind increases or decreases since the sighter shot and adjust your aim accordingly. Dance with the wind, enjoy it when the breeze pushes a shot into the middle of your group.

# 9

# *Advanced Wind Shooting*

The conditions prevalent during the match and aggregate often dictate the technique used to shoot a group.

### Slow Fire Technique.

This is used on those still mornings or evenings when there is the barest of wind movement and you'll have no problem getting off all the shots in the time limit. Aim at exactly the same place for each shot, be aware of disturbing the sandbags as little as possible during reloading. Carefully adjust the crosshairs with the screw on the front pedestal before the next shot. Wait for the exact same amount of flag deflection before pulling the trigger again.

Some use this style in just the opposite condition, the day when the wind is so strong the flags spend most of their time doing a clothesline imitation. Again, the rifle is settled and the shot isn't fired till the proper amount of sag shows on a key flag. On the really windy days a ribbon gets overpowered. The best thing then is wind socks like Bob DeMonstoy of Painted Post, New York uses. A perfect example of the slow fire technique during an early morning calm occurred the first time I shot 300 yards, at the Stittsville range, in Ontario, Canada. It was an overcast day; during the warm up match there was the faintest amount of wind movement from 4:00 over our shoulders. After two sighter shots touched, the first two record shots were carefully squeezed off: they formed a small dot in the top half of the 300 yard bull. Taking my time, very carefully reloading and returning to battery, adjusting the rear bag for perfect aim the third shot didn't make the hole any bigger. Repeat the process and the fourth shot went into the same bug hole. There's now a square four shot hole at 300 yards that measures

*Jim Novak shows off his .446″ 300 yard IBS Record. Shot through some tough mirage in the middle of the day; Jim threw down a group that stayed at the top of the heap for several years.*

.263″. Even in a 36X Leupold that looks tiny. Being a rookie, I made a rookie mistake and jumped from the bench in excitement after the fourth shot. By the time I settled back at the bench for the fifth shot the calm was gone, a very slight strengthening of the wind over the shoulder influenced the last shot to produce an officially measured .520″ group. Still, a fine effort and good use of the slow fire technique. By the way, ask Fletcher Williams who shot the second smallest group that day.

### Rapid Fire Technique

The second major shooting technique is rapid fire. The keys are.
1. Speed - If the brass ain't flying you're dying
2. Use the record shots as sighters. Be aware of the flags while you're reloading, or bent over and peering through the scope. If the wind picks up or lets off and moves the impact chase the next shot into the condition. Figure out where the next shot will go before pulling the trigger.
3. You MUST be willing to stop on a radical shift of the flags. Pay attention with your off eye, watch while reloading. After pausing, wait for the condition to return, go to the sighter and start all over again.
   The best piece of advice for a good rapid fire group is to start in the right condition. Test conditions in the warm up and early in the match. Go with a

winner. Fletcher Williams got into a condition a few years ago at the Super Shoot. He plunked down three good groups at 200 yards and exclaimed more than once to all who would listen (and a few who wouldn't) "I'm going to run that condition if it kills me". As I recall he had to search for it, but found a hole after those last two groups and thumped us proper that day.

He did what a lot of competitors do, especially at 200. Run a record string during a wind trend. This is the build, peak, decline cycle. If the first shot is at the start of a cycle the aim is adjusted into the pickup for the next shot. Slightly more into additional pickup for the third shot, hold back out as the wind decreases and then as the condition dies the same hold as the first shot for the last. Four different aiming points produce one hole on the edge of the bull.

This process of holding off is especially important when working with the sighter during your string. It's whether to hold off the full value as shown on the sighter or less than that amount. It's a matter of attitude. Do you want to win, or place in the top 50%. To win at the National level you need to trust your equipment and judgement of the flags. At 200 yards if the flags and sighter say to hold on the eight ring, two inches away from the group, be confident and do it. Using my skeletal aluminum stocked Light Varmint I shot a five shot 200 yard group of .134″ at Johnstown, New York in 1985. Early in a match the first three record shots were in a left to right trickle, they piled into a dot just outside the 10 ring. Through a 36X scope the group was estimated at less than .200″. Then came a full reverse that lasted several minutes. Sighter testing showed this a perfect condition also, though from another direction. The new impact point was on the opposite side of the moth ball. Holding on the outside of the eight ring I piled in the last two shots in a complete reverse. To prove it wasn't a fluke the three sighter shots to test the new condition measure .155″ at 200 yards. Practice, gain confidence, hold the full value and work for the best group possible.

## Lost Shots Before or During the Group

Displaced shots are the nemesis of group shooting. They can come from poor equipment, technique, or missed conditions. Here we'll discuss the ones caused by the wind. If a shot is fired it's expected to go into the group. Very few triggers get pulled to ruin things on purpose. When they don't go in there are several things to do.

1. Immediately look down range and try to identify the flags that explain the bullet movement. If it's an intensity change use the last shot as a sighter and hold the next one.
2. If the wind intensity's the same - did a head wind or tail wind angle change move the impact up or down? Again, use this new knowledge and adjust the aim for the next shot.

*Some days it all comes together and you end up on top. Bob DeMonstoy hands Bob White a trophy at Painted Post.*

When the first shot in the string pops up a good group can still be saved by chasing with subsequent shots. Check with a sighter shot and make sure the new point of impact isn't from a wind condition change you missed. If you chase a high shot without checking and put another even higher there's no one to blame but the loose nut behind the butt. Shooting in the 1982 IBS Nationals I had Heavy Varmint 100 sewn up through four groups. In windy and switching conditions I wasted a .169″ on the warm up. The first four record matches were .224″, .212″, .158″, and .254″. I knew if I threw down another .250″ it would be an easy victory. Shooting from the dangerous, upwind, bench one; Pete Rechnitzer - another lefty sat next to me on bench number two for that fifth match. The first record shot popped up above the moth ball when all previous shots had been below the moth ball. I slammed two sighters down to check it and they went into that high area. Back to the record target, and firing rapidly, the next two went into a tiny hole to make a .100″ three shot group. The fourth dropped straight out the bottom to about .300″ and the fifth blew me out of the water when it went down to the original impact point and made a group of .374″. Fourth place in the aggregate at the Nationals isn't so bad. Well, yes it is when the opportunity for first slips by on the fifth shot. It turned out Pete had been watching the flags while I ran the string. He pointed out the flags that turned while I was speeding without a license. The moral of the story is: I started the group without knowing which flags had caused the impact point to move above the mothball, with closer attention the group and aggregate could easily have been saved.

When the impact moves left or right a flag down range will usually explain the movement and it's easy to chase the shot. If your observation says the shot should impact the group and it doesn't you have some work to do. Use the sighter to find the indicator that explains that shot.

## Adjusting to Changing Conditions

Several specific types of conditions could appear during the course of a shoot. A match is a trigger pull when an overcast sky and very light breezes let you aim at the same place for every shot. In these matches you feel you're losing ground on the leaders if the target comes back a .229″ at 100 or .545″ at 200. In equipment shoots like this take time to settle your rifle completely. If a shot gets touched off with the crosshairs slightly out of the group the target scorer won't let you try again.

Conditions go from the easy trigger pull up to the most difficult. The most difficult are rapidly swirling gusts where mirage keeps sighter and record shots from being visible. Lots of different conditions are available. The key to adapting to the days conditions is being aware of what's possible during a relay, and what are the prevailing conditions. Go to the line before your relay. Study wind direction and velocity, time the wind cycles. How long does a gust take to switch, build, peak, decline, and switch. Would you get off five shots? three? two? Pick the predominant condition and test it on the sighter. Sometimes here are the good groups easily, although much of the time the shorter non-normal condition is gentler and gives the better group. If that's the case you'll have to test your nerve and wait for it, and wait, and wait. Know how long you can delay and still finish the string. One minute forty five seconds, one minute, forty seconds? KNOW the limit by testing with a stopwatch. I use an inexpensive Casio sports watch with a built in forward and reverse timer in it. Have your stopwatch at the bench and running during all matches. The range officer doesn't always give the commands on time. The stopwatch makes your willingness to wait calculated rather than a gamble. NBRSA gives no finishing commands other than two minutes, one minute and cease fire. How can you wait those last few precious seconds on a decreasing condition if you don't know how much time is left? When shooting NBRSA matches I set the alarm to go off five seconds before the cease fire command. Then if I hear it I know it's time to pull the trigger no matter what the wind is doing.

Repeat your observations and calculations during the day. The best time killer during the five relays at the Super Shoot is to pick a few good shooters from each relay. Select some who shoot the same bench rotation; watch them through a spotting scope before your relay for invaluable information. You can usually tell where they held each shot by following the sighter. I'm

*Paul Ryan shows off five tiny targets. On an overcast day with no wind the biggest target isn't very big.*

easy to watch. Before any record shots I'll test on the sighter. Anytime a record string gets interrupted there is always a sighter shot to check impact before another record. Allie Euber is tough to watch, he's a good enough wind doper he patterns the conditions early and doesn't always check the sighter late in the relay, even when you know he's firing in conditions he hasn't been using. Jerry Masker isn't a good choice, poor eyesight has forced him to become a marvelous wind doper who rarely goes back for sighter shots. (Allie calls him one of the best wind dopers ever, high praise indeed.) Lester Bruno shoots so many sighters you can't tell which mean anything. I like to follow him anyway. High drama unfolds at the end of the relay when he runs out of time. Watching also gives the opportunity to observe switches the shooter doesn't catch after they dip their head to the scope. (Keep the off eye open.) You don't make any friends though by going up to them afterwards and saying: "Boy are you dumb, I saw that switch just before you shot". Some of my other favorites to watch include Don Geraci, Gary Ocock, Bob White, Myles Hollister, PJ Hart, Doc Maretzo, Dennis Wagner, Lowell Frei and whichever cute entrants Doc Palmisano brought.

The Tomball range near Houston, Texas is notorious for starting the day left to right, out of the cool trees, and ending right to left, across the baked flats. When things switch figure out where your best group is and go get it.

*Compare the angles of the flags in these two pictures. Taken 10 seconds apart you can easily see the valuable information wind flags give to a benchrest shooter.*

## Uncommon Wind Indicators

For the same reasons shooters go to the line early and observe prevalent conditions you have to expand your focus to include some uncommon indicators. I can still picture Phil Sauer at the 1982 IBS National. He would stand behind the line at Kelbly's, rocked backed the way he likes, with a studious expression looking down range at the variables in the wind pattern. (You can use big words like variable and studious when you speak of an experimenter like Phil.) His study that year yielded the Three-Gun Crown.

The classic example of uncommon indicators has been repeated many times. A shooter waits for a strand of grass in front of the target to bend just the correct amount and a winning group appears while those around him shoot wailing wall rejects (also called shotgun patterns, weather reports, @#%*X!V&* etc). Let's open our horizons even further. How many of you look at the trees far up range on a gusty day to see when a calm will hold for thirty seconds. This works at Kelbly's range in Ohio. Two groves of trees several hundred yards upwind have helped me out on numerous occasions (this must mean the wind blows in Ohio if I've needed them on several occasions). Camillus, New York is another range where the line of trees that extends far upwind can keep trouble at bay. Sitting next to Wally Hart in a varmint match at Camillus I was happy as a clam waiting for a slack to come in. With no shots on record and time running down Wally suggested I glance way up range. Looking up, trees were bent over from an approaching cloudburst, fingers blurred, and the brass sparkled as it flew through the air. The Black Canyon Range north of Phoenix, Arizona has a big bore range several hundred yards upwind. Those 20 foot high range flags are a perfect indicator of conditions on their way.

When you're shooting on the down wind side of the range the best time to start a string is when the flags from up wind switch over and steady in the angle and velocity you've been looking for. The upwind range flags give plenty of warning about intensity increases or decreases, all you have to watch out for is reverses sneaking in from the back side.

A favorite tip is listening to the moans and groans of those around you. If your neighbor screams, pulls his hair, curses, and throws his bolt down range don't touch off a shot. Let the gust, letup, or mirage boil settle and throw a few sighter shots down range. (Speaking of throwing things - once I left an MTM box, full of 6BR cases, on top of the Camillus clubhouse roof.)

Be aware of the swirls and eddies around you. Breeze from behind hasn't had a chance to move flags but can be the most important on its influence on bullet flight. Topography influences wind in the same fashion the ground influences water. Thermal influences dictate that conditions generally move downhill in the cooler evening, and morning hours. Then when there's enough warming the conditions tend to move uphill. This changeover presents a completely different set of patterns for the shooter. By being observant you'll notice a few other peculiarities. In a protected range like Johnstown a light breeze moving from left to right will spill over the top of the trees, then eddy back towards the base of the trees with a few moments of reverse for the first ten benches, before the condition strengthens enough to wash out the eddy and show left to right over the whole range. The same thing happens around large man made objects. The Central Jersey range, Kelbly's, and New Braunfels all show the same effect. Boy does it drive you nuts when you don't know what's causing it, or when it's not readable.

Read this chapter several times. Understanding the effect of wind on a bullet is the most important item in the book for a beginning accuracy buff. Once you believe in the wind moving the bullet half the task of a good aggregate is completed.

# 10

# *Wind Flags*

Modern wind flag designs, and the proper use of them, has been as much of the reason for todays excellent shooting as equipment. When a shooter goes to the range without wind indicators to put down range they are in essence arriving with only one. The wind felt on the body is the only indicator to rely on. Other objects down range can give small bits of information, because of their movement in the breeze, but there's nothing quantifiable. Shooting an accurate rifle without wind flags is playing a game of chance. Shots out of the group might be the fault of a gust which passed the 50 yard mark just as the shot went off, or they might be the fault of the rifle. WITHOUT WIND FLAGS YOU'RE WASTING TIME AND EFFORT.

The chapters on shooting in the wind explored the physics involved in the movement of a bullet. It explained that movement is quantifiable. Stronger wind moves the bullet further; lesser breezes move it less. With wind flags, sighter shots, and proper hold over, the modern shooter has a chance to keep all the shots in a cluster even in tough conditions. Just using sighter shots alone doesn't give enough information for calculated hold over. Has the wind picked up or decreased since that sighter shot of a few seconds ago? By having wind flags out in front of the bench the holding decision is a decision rather than a guess. When you're shooting a big match with lots of flags it's easy to see approaching gusts, letups, or switches. Trained fingers can easily insert the new round while you rotate your eyes uprange, downrange, then out in front. Look uprange for gusts which will arrive before you get a chance to shoot; look downrange for switches which are trying to sneak in the back door and influence a shot. Look out front for the condition you've been using and check if it's ok for another shot or if you need to go back to the sighter.

*Marcy Lyons adjusts a wind flag so it's visible in the bottom of the sight picture. It's an easy way to see reverses after you dip your head to peer through the scope.*

Shooting alone at the range we don't get the full field flag coverage that gives such a good read on the conditions. The absolute minimum anytime you're at the range is one flag 20 yards in front of the bench. One flag is better than none, but it leaves big gaps downrange for gusts and letups. I prefer a minimum of three flags: one at 20, one at 40, and one at 70 yards. The wind on your body is the fourth indicator so this set-up gives good coverage right out in front. Think back to some of the things we discussed in the wind shooting chapter. Conditions have the most effect on bullet flight when the bullet's at its greatest rate of velocity loss, which is close to the muzzle, this means the immediate flags are the most important. If you've got the time (and the flags) put out a flag 20 yards upwind, and 20 yards downwind of each of the main string. Extra flags give warning about incoming conditions.

Wind flags come in three main types with several possible variations and combinations of each. The first type is the basic ribbon. Prepared from three quarters to one inch colorful cloth ribbon, or bright orange surveyors tape; ribbon flags are most usable in light, quickly changing conditions up to four or five miles per hour. A slight difference, either in direction or velocity, in a trickling condition is quickly apparent to sensitive ribbon flags. These flags are most usable in the first 100 yards of the range. After 100 yards small streamers aren't visible enough and can give misleading information as to wind velocity and direction. To improve visibility, and reliably show direction, ribbons are added to wind vanes made of light-weight material like balsa. By painting these vanes a different primary color on each side wind direction changes are visible much further down range.

The second main type of wind flag is the "daisy wheel". A daisy wheel is an adaptation of the yellow plastic revolving daisy used for lawn decorations. The molded daisy is removed from the simple bent rod on which it had been supported. With the addition of a guiding wind vane out the back, a bearing in the center of the daisy to spin on, a bearing on top of the movable stand on which it rotates, and some black paint on three of the petals to help show rate of spin, the shooter has a classy and reliable wind indicator. Modified daisies come into their own anytime the wind picks up past a slight breeze. They're highly visible when used in the second half of a 200 yard match, beating plain ribbons hands down at the longer distances.

Combinations always seem to be popular with daisies, vanes, and ribbons being added to the same stand. Like any other operation in life, once we go beyond a certain complexity the information derived might be more confusing than helpful. On any mechanical flag simplicity, balance, and accurate response is more important than anything. The worst types of flags are those devised with pointers attached to some form of a pendulum which is assumed to gage the level of the wind. A flat part of the indicator is supposed to be pushed by the wind, point to a certain number, and attest how far to hold over. Problems crop up in actual usage since the winds blowing across any outside range are never constant. These things start to flap, (like a broken winged goose before a retriever latches on), as soon as the wind hits them. In a struggle between the relentless, consistent pull of gravity, and the intermittent, fluid push of the breeze the wind never wins out. Another serious design fault is daisy wheels where the vane isn't large enough to accurately track the device into the wind. When the wind blows on a daisy where the petals have as much surface area as the vane it gets the whole thing wiggling like a drunk on Saturday night. I guess the flag owner decided there was so much time and effort in constructing them they might as well put them downrange anyway, even though they give false information.

Keep the indicators large enough to see at the distances where they're placed. I'm always amazed when I'm walking downrange, placing flags at the 75 yard mark, when I see contraptions with tiny indicators and little model airplane propellers in place of a daisy. Whoever's using them would have to set up a spotting scope on each one to get any usable information off them that far from the firing line.

The third major alternative is the wind sock. I've always found tubes difficult to read in light to medium conditions, but wind socks can put the pancakes on the table during extremely windy conditions. When the wind is really screaming across the range light flags, and daisies, can be over-

*Two of the popular styles for wind flags. A modified daisy and a streamer.*

powered. Because of their 45 degree petal angle the daisies get to a certain rpm and a gust can't noticeably accelerate them any more. Light ribbons don't give any useful information if they're stretched straight out from the pole; here's the time when the sock will pay its dues. Small socks about three feet long with a three to five inch opening will show the exact point to trigger a shot. When the sock fills and points straight out it will always "break" at a certain wind velocity as the gust lets up. By watching the sock for the correct directional angle, and triggering a shot just after the sock breaks, you'll hold together a better group than anyone who's trying to read an overpowered daisy.

Stand design is dependent on your requirements. If you have a backdoor range like the one Ed Goff has the flag stands become permanent. (Ed says his shooting bench is right under the kitchen window - drives his wife nuts every time he triggers a shot just as she passes the window.) When flags are used at the local public range, or if you travel to lots of away matches, something more portable than the Rock of Gibralter is in order. Music stands seem to be one of the popular, though more expensive, options. With a triangular base that has room for a rock weight strong winds won't blow them over.

Several ranges of adjustment help fit the stand to the local topography and get the flag up to the bottom of the target, near the line of bullet flight. Pointed metal tubes that can be driven into the ground are fine as long as the

*Here's an expensive flag with several design faults. The vane isn't large enough to track steadily into the wind. A fixed pointer doesn't work when the wind angle changes.*

tip where the pounding hammer strikes isn't the same place the pivot is supposed to ride upon. For different height options build the stand in two pieces, one shorter than the other, if it's possible. Ranges like Kelbly's and Johnstown, New York have a crown in them between the firing line and the targets. If your flags don't go low enough for the shooters on all the relays they get placed on the ground by the referees. Bob Adamowicz has made the most beautiful flags. With a large vane covered in heat shrink model airplane wing material, his very sensitive and well-balanced flags never lied to me any time I used them. Problem was, on tall stands, at the Johnstown range they didn't do any good sitting flat after being pulled. (Trying hard you could still read them on the ground, but it took one heck of a gust to get the daisy to spin!)

On ranges where shooters rotate benches between matches the rules state flags must be below the line-of-sight to the sighter portion of the target. Hey all you right handed shooters, remember us lefties shoot from the other side of the bench. During setup, when you're checking through the scope for clearance, move the rests to the other side of the bench and make sure it's clear on that side. Cecil Tucker and I got acquainted at a Tomball match when I put a 68 grain boat tail into his carefully machined wind flag. I had switched the scope over from Light Varmint to Heavy Varmint and bore sighted before the sight-in period. Cecil was shooting the first relay, with me following on the second. He had set up his fine flags so they were visible in the bottom of his scope. Anyone who has done much bore sighting knows it's easy to be six inches off on the first shot at 100 yards. Well as it so happened the beautiful machined head of Cecil's flag was six inches below the bull on the sighter target. You know what happened - I fired that first shot and it didn't hit the paper! Double checking the bore sight I put in a few clicks up and the next shot hit the bottom of the target. Continuing merrily on, the group in great conditions was a nice tidy "one". Cecil came up after the first relay had shot its first record match and asked (with a scowl) "did you shoot my wind flag?" I didn't know this guy (Cecil's one of those big Texas boys) all I knew was the first shot hadn't hit the paper, it was too low. Cecil's a good old boy and wasn't really mad (I think) when we got it all straightened out. As it turned out he picked up the pieces of his flag the next break, sure enough there was a severe bend in the flag stand and a bullet splash in the center of the flag head. What a way to get introduced, since then we've become good shooting friends at the matches.

Bob White, Jim Novak, and I always had great fun designing playful wind flags. As a group we chortled and giggled like the characters in the comic strip "Calvin and Hobbes" while creating radio controlled flags which would do all sorts of wonderful things while the competitors were waiting for the range officer to give the commence fire command. My favorite from one windy year at the Super Shoot was the daisy which would spin so fast it would take off with a whoosh and climb into the sky. (Now who would want to throw everyone on the line into a blue funk with a flag like that! I would probably trigger that one when Fletcher Williams came to the line - just to see him spout.)

# 11

# *Mirage*

Warren Page described trying for a good target when the mirage is running as: "Shooting through the swimming pool". A vivid description of what it's like holding together a group on days when the mirage is making it difficult to see 6mm bullet holes at 200 yards. You don't have to be in this game very long before running into a day where a 6mm bullet hole planted into a 200 yard target ring is invisible. Days where it's at its worst, mirage makes it hard to see bullet holes at 100 yards!

Webster's Dictionary describes mirage as: "A reflection visible at sea, in deserts, or above a hot pavement of some distant object often in distorted form as a result of atmospheric conditions". The key words are the: "the result of atmospheric conditions". In shooting we're concerned with the fact that light passes through still air and liquids straight, but when it goes through a combination of the two it gets bent. It's actually straight lines with kinks where it hits different combinations.

The mirage we see through a scope is the deflection of light waves passing through different densities of poorly mixed air and water vapor. Differences in both density and humidity can cause changes. Cool air is more dense than warm air, as the sun heats the air close to the ground it moves upwards through the cooler air just above it. When it rises with no horizontal components we get those nice little bubbles which cause the sight picture to bounce. With the addition of some wind drift there's lateral movement as well. Thrown into the equation is the effect of different humidity. When those "bubbles" start to move they bring the moist air close the ground with them. You want to talk about a good time to get sighter suckered, this is it. There's so much going on at the same time the condition never stays readable for two shots in a row. This misdirection of

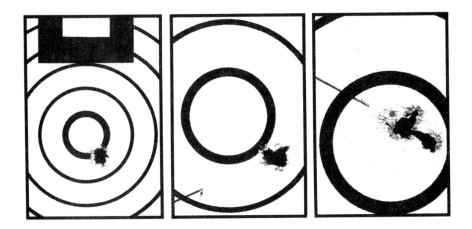

*The authors three smallest targets shot in competition, shown exact size. A .074" at 100 yards; .134" at 200 yards; .520" at 300 yards.*

light waves causes problems for the shooter trying to finish a good group as the bull expands, distorts, and bobs up and down like an apple in a water barrel.

Tests on counteracting mirage by playing with optics have never proven beneficial. Several devices with changeable irises which attached to the eyepiece of the scope were intended to give some benefit by knocking out the apparent mirage effect. Along the same lines many chose to switch to a lower power scope during days of bad mirage. By switching to a 20X or 24X scope the reasoning was the bull would be more obvious since the mirage wouldn't be as visible. These things were all proven to be a detriment rather than a help. Use a 36X scope, invest in a couple of mirage boards to show mirage flow direction, and shoot to the best of your ability. The mirage board gives a good indication of the intensity of the "waves". With a board in place on each side of the target you won't have to keep switching your focus to the top of the target frame for an idea of the pace of the mirage flow. You can't hold for what you can't see. When it takes a group in the "threes" or "fours" to win a 200 yard match nowadays, in order to have enough information, you need that high powered scope to see which side of the group is being impacted by the shots.

I can offer a few words of advice about what to do in bad mirage. First is to remember that a bullet losing speed faster is more wind sensitive. The bullet is at its highest rate of loss right after leaving the barrel. Put the greatest weight into the wind and mirage indicators which are closer to the firing line. Many of the rimfire shooters will have a spotting scope which they focus on the mirage to help get a good read. Some of the things I've noticed: there is often a lag between when the mirage flips over, and when the flags show the change. I've always been a wind flag dominated shooter. I'll pay attention to the mirage and make sure it's flipped and is holding steady, then wait for the wind to build so I don't catch a sudden reverse or boil, then touch off the shot. It's always tough to know where to hold on days when the mirage is running so heavy the bull looks like it's distorted to two or three times its normal width. There can be horizontal, the left or right push of the wind; and vertical, the bubbles of heated air, components in the sight picture. The only trick I've latched on to which has proven consistent is to pay strict attention to the wind flags and dope when to touch off a shot. Since the mirage is distorting the bull excessively it's harder to know exactly where to aim. Here's the trick: "Aim and shoot at the point the bull snaps back to". Reread that last sentence and analyze it on a piece of paper, then check it next time you're at the range. Set up on a solid rest and look through the scope without touching the rifle: when the mirage is running horizontally the bull seems to elongate and move in a direction downwind. Watching carefully you'll notice that when the bull stretches downwind it never goes to exactly the same point every time, the conditions effecting the sight picture are variable: they move it more or less depending on strength. You'll also notice that when the bull snaps back at the end of a particular push it seems to go back to almost the same place every time. Dope the wind off the flags and aim at that spot. It usually takes a little luck but I've dumped some great groups down range using that technique. The best I can remember is a .080″ group in Light Varmint at the 1981 IBS Nationals in Johnstown. The morning aggregate was running a little slow, by the time the fifth record came around it was past lunch time. With the crown in the range Johnstown can produce prodigious amounts of mirage. The ground is so close to the line of bullet flight it's easy to get a bubble through just as a shot is touched off. On the .080″ I held where I thought the bull was and touched off the shots based on the gently moving flags. There was enough mirage running that through the scope the group looked like a .150″ when it was all done, the mirage was distorting it to double its size. Like I said it takes some luck, but good groups are possible in tough conditions.

Days where the mirage is thick as pea soup put a test to the temperament of any shooter. At 100 yards mirage is an inconvenience but it's usually manageable. It's at 200 yards and beyond where we all pull out clumps of hair. If the rifle was sighted in earlier for 100 the switch to 200 isn't too difficult. It's the days where there's been a scope switch we get into trouble. Be extra fine with the bore sight, and the only time I'll put one into a stainless barrel, consider using a collimeter if there's no warm-up match.

Two hints for what to do when you can't see shots at 200 yards. First is to watch through the scope for 15-20 seconds after the shot. Clarity will get better or worse depending on the flow. Often it's a matter of waiting a few seconds for a change, then the shot becomes visible. The other thing to try, especially if the first shot landed on a ring, is to shoot another with the same hold. The next shot isn't likely to land smack in the middle of the ring again, so it's visible. When this disappearing act happens I'll shoot a clump of three to make sure of point of impact.

Talk to everyone you can about how they dope the mirage. Get bull sessions going with your neighbor while you're both looking through the scope before the commence fire command. Read the mirage chapter in THE ACCURATE RIFLE and any other target shooting book. Experiment with everything you learn, find which techniques give the best results, then persevere. Remember, everyone else is having just as much trouble.

# 12

# Practice and Competition

It's hard to practice for competition without an accurate rifle and load. To really learn how to use the wind, flags, and sighter target the rifle must be a shooter. For the best results you need confidence the combination is the best available, otherwise, when it tosses a shot you won't trust the flags. That's what you need to do. Believe the wind, mirage, or hold is pushing out every shot that didn't go into one hole.

## Goals

At the beginning of every season, and before every match, set goals for yourself. Early on, while you're gaining experience, they must be achievable. I wonder if Gary Ocock's ears are ringing but beating him in individual groups was my first goal. By concentrating on him alone, and watching group by group over a long period of time, I had a few each weekend smaller than his. If, every time you go to a match you only compare with the one who's winning it's discouraging. Realize the leaders will be different each week and ignore them for a while. My goals early on were to beat Gary, Bob White, Jim Novak, Joe Ambrose, and his wife Joan. You know about Gary, I was trying to beat the others because we were all loading under the same tarpaulin and betting a quarter a group. It get's expensive unless you win two groups a day. After reaching the first easy goals it's time for something harder to achieve. In my case, the next goal was to win a trophy at a registered match. My first registered match was the wonderful event the Stonewall Rifle and Pistol Club used to put on in Staunton, Virginia: the birthplace of Woodrow Wilson, a nice little town of 25,000. An early April event has to be south of the snow line. That's where I got my first taste of Mello Yello. (Well that was the mixer anyway. This stuff was

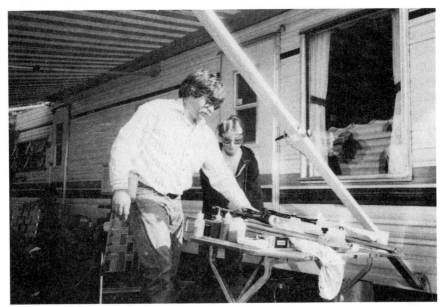

*Jim Novak and Joan Ambrose show off a comfortable set-up for matches.*
*Trailers with awnings have lots of room for cleaning and loading areas.*

similar to Rebel Yell, but it came in a clear bottle with a screw top.) With
only a Heavy Varmint rifle I was limited to shooting one class. As it turned
out, in the grand aggregate I was 54th out of 55 shooters. My small group at
100 yards was a .370″, largest group was 2.670″ (loose scope). Small group
at 200 yards was 1.151″, largest was 2.860″ (no loose scope, maybe a loose
nut) for a grand aggregate of .9980″. I whitewashed a guy using a Tasco
scoped Remington 700 BDL in .22-250. Jeanne Lynn, one of my favorite
shooters, was hot that weekend. At 100 yards she shot five shot groups of
.189″, .221″, .252″, .389″ and .303″ for first in the range aggregate. At 200
yards she shot .615″, .945″, .784″, .754″, and .546″ for another range
aggregate victory. After shooting a first and a first guess who won the
Heavy Varmint Grand Aggregate?

It took 14 grand aggregates before a trophy materialized. At the August
Mainville match, so I wouldn't sit around in the afternoon, I also entered
my 6BR Heavy Varmint rifle in the Heavy Bench Class. Shooting every
week since April with Bob White had shortened my learning curve. That
weekend in August all the practice, and week after week of competition
came together with a nice .2622 range aggregate for a win in 200 yard
Heavy Varmint. Also won were the 200 yard Heavy Bench Aggregate, and
the Heavy Bench Grand Aggregate. The last trophy of the weekend was for
the HV/HB 2-gun. A .4596 HV/HB 2-Gun Aggregate out-paced Bob
Demonstoy and his second place .5551.

The confidence from achieving attainable goals allows a shooter to set higher goals. My belief is to set several easy to accomplish goals, several that must be worked for, and a few that are just unbelievable. The unbelievable ones are often accomplished after they're placed on paper and contemplated during the year. New goals for this season have been staring me in the face since the end of the November. For a seasoned shooter goals might include: winning a range aggregate, or grand aggregate. For a top flight competitor it might be to do the same at a major. Winning the IBS Three Gun Championship and Rookie of the Year in 1981 gave me the confidence to set high goals for 1982.

My 1982 goals were: to place top five in one class at the IBS Nationals, and make the IBS International Postal Team. To Make top 20 in the Three-Gun, to set one IBS International Record, to win $100.00 at the Super Shoot, to win a grand aggregate at a registered match. To make Top 10 in two of the three classes at the IBS 200-300 Yard Championships, to make Top 20 in all three classes at the IBS Nationals, and to achieve enough points for the IBS Precision Rifleman Award. These goals are all achievable for a hot shooter. I believed they were all a distinct possibility. The outrageous goal for the year was to win all four range aggregates at a registered match.

Some of these goals came easily: the grand aggregate, a Light Varmint win first match of the year at Staunton, Virginia. The $100.00 was a 200 yard .247" Heavy Varmint group using my 10 1/2 pound Light Varmint. The IBS Record was oh so near. Three times targets went for official measure, all three times someone else was a little smaller for the weekend and they got the record. The goals for the Nationals were all met. The Precision Rifleman award came up one point short, it had to wait for the second match in 1983. The only goal really missed was the lofty one. Using that 10 1/2 pounder I won both Heavy Varmint aggregates at Mainville in June, but Light Varmint was third and sixth. That was the best effort for the season. The worst placing for the year was at the Super Shoot. Using a .22/45 with a shell holder bolt face I was 105th and 107th in Unlimited (guess where I finished? Wrong - I was 108th) 75th and 15th in Heavy Varmint for 31st in the Grand.

For 1989 My goals are: win a major, shoot a Light Varmint 100 yard aggregate below .1600, set one record, Shoot a .1900 200 yard aggregate, win $500 at the Super Shoot, and get four points toward the Benchrest Hall of Fame. Of course include the Grand Slam which has never come closer than three out of four. These are noble goals. I may not achieve half of them but tough goals provide teeth gritting, fiery eyed, intensity during practice and competition.

Goals lead directly into the next phase of practice and competition. Mental preparedness. The goals provide a base from which to prepare for a shooting session. No matter how good a shooter is there will be days when

*Walt Berger, the NBRSA President, sets up for another small group.*

all the shots don't go into one hole. To become discouraged is an acceptance of defeat. Next to having an accurate rifle my largest concern before a big match is mental preparedness and visualization exercises. I use a great deal of visualization during the time I'm not at the range. Here in Houston we spend lots of time on the freeways. I watch flags on the highway, tumbling wrappers, the mirage run off a car top, heat waves across a parking lot. In my mind I see the clunk of brass hitting a bench top, a fast reload and crosshair alignment, a gradual wind change building, being held for, and a shot in the middle of a bug hole. Fix in your mind that no matter what happens this firing line is where you want to be. If the group gets too big, well, that's part of benchrest. Perseverance when things aren't going right will pay dividends later on in the match, aggregate, or season. 1985 is my best example of mental preparedness leading to match success. That year was a rough one for match attendance, the total for the year was only six events. These included two Heavy Bench club matches, the Super Shoot, one registered match at Council Cup in June, the IBS 200/300 yard Championships at Mainville, and the IBS Varmint Nationals. Unable to practice during the off weekends, to do well I needed to get my head screwed on before travelling to an event. The 100 yard groups showed how the preparedness paid off. The whole season saw only one group that measured .400″ or above. There were more groups that measured less than .200″ than over .300″. With a couple of "Official Screamers" thrown in it was a good year at 100 yards. The same results were evident at 200 yards. Discounting the severe wind scouring the range during the 200/300 Nationals in Heavy Varmint, 24 out of the 39 200 yard groups that year were less than .700″. For the first time since 1982 I went into the IBS Nationals having confidence I was about to win a major event. That feeling was the first step to winning the Light Varmint/Heavy Varmint 2-Gun.

Whatever your level of skill, and experience, include having fun in any list of mental preparation. We enjoy this game for many reasons. Let's compare it to a marriage. In the union of two there must be love to carry on when infatuation and lust diminish. If we include fun in Benchrest it carries us through the years in the beginning when the trophy's are few and far between. It helps keep us humble when the pieces of flesh and steel act in unison to produce record groups, and winning aggregates. And it again carries us in our later years when the trophies are few and far between. Art Blensinger, Dan Hufnail, John Bunch, and Homer Culver have been fine shooters for many years. I guarantee they have fun shooting the bull, and the bullets with their friends.

Never put the bulk of your practice into the beautiful conditions found early in the morning and late in the evening. These super conditions are fine for verifying the load is accurate, but they don't do any good for competitive practice. I've only heard of one or two times where a match was delayed because of too much wind or rain. Before the change of rules, when you were disqualified if a shot went outside the border, there were 38 out of 52 shooters disqualified at one 200 yard match. I shot a 300 yard Light Varment target, in Canada, where all five bullets hit outside the border. There was another time in gusty, switching, winds where I was holding shots on either side, outside the 200 yard border, and praying they would hit somewhere on the paper. These are extreme examples, but they show you must be aware of how to handle some rough conditions. Real terrible conditions create a perfect time to maintain a competitive edge and move up to the top of the list. My good friend Bobby Hart, of Robert W. Hart and Son in Nescopeck, Pennsylvania, came through in 1985 with an IBS 300 yard Heavy Varmint Championship, by persevering when others had given up, on a windy weekend at Mainville. His 300 yard five shot groups measured 3.050″, 2.052″, 1.783″ (maybe he should get an Official Screamer patch for that one), 4.383″, and 2.755″. With those groups he won! One of my friends, a Hall of Fame member from up north, shot a group within 1/2″ of either side of a 10.5″ target. I shouldn't make fun, I DQ'd on the first record match and followed that up with groups of 2.964″, 5.200″, 3.952″, and 6.700″. What a weekend, I wasted a perfectly good 2.945″ on the warm-up.

Small groups and aggregates are the sum of many correct choices. In competition these choices come easier if they have been previously observed in practice. During practice sessions use a stop watch to estimate the

*Sometimes everything goes right. Glenn Newick shows off the IBS Three-Gun Trophy he won in 1981.*

time to reload and get back on target. Run one, two, three, four, and five shot strings; check each against the twitching second hand. Be smooth in every phase of loading, and aiming. Get the cases close to the loading port, be comfortable so it's not a stretch to reload. Gradually build speed to get the shot string off in one condition. Use good technique while reloading, train both hands for speed. To include both hands to their best advantage the fastest action style for a right hander has a right handed bolt with a left handed loading port. This style has an added advantage with the loading port right in front of your eyes.

Don't lever the bell of the scope while opening the bolt, if you need leverage put your thumb on the mount. To get back on target quickly disturb the rifle as little as possible in the bags. If the neck sized cases are too tight and require excessive pressure to open or close the bolt, full length resize just enough the bolt opens and closes easier. Even when you're hurrying a string be positive the crosshairs are exactly where they're supposed to be. One shot thrown will spoil the other four, no matter how good they are. The most common saying at any match is: "The first four were in a bug hole". Sometimes muzzle blast in the vicinity, for one reason or another, causes one of those shots to step out of the group. Notice the rhythm of the shooters on either side. If there's plenty of time you can do several things. One of the easiest if you can rapid fire is to wait till your wing men have finished their string, otherwise time your shots in between theirs. When I'm running out

*The wailing wall hears the same words over and over: "I had the first four shots in a bug hole". Dwight Scott and Paul Johnson peer at some of the 200 yard groups at the Cactus Classic.*

of time I pay no attention to anything but fast sighter shots, faster reloads, and analyzing the flags for where to hold the record shots. Think back after finishing one of these rushed groups. The level of concentration you achieved probably blocked out all the outside distractions. With no influence from the shots and talking around you the group probably held together. That's the level of concentration you're trying to achieve in the important groups.

Bench etiquette demands some common courtesy. If you're done with your group, don't play with the sighter, in the last minute, while the next bench is struggling to put the last shot into a group. Don't yell out: "Look at the bug-hole on bench eight" while someone is trying to finish out a group. They have enough pressure as it is.

You increase the worth of your practice and build skill as a marksman by calling each shot before, and after, it's fired. Estimate how much the wind will move the bullet whether you're on the sighter or record. Be aware of the position of the cross hairs when the shot is fired. Factor in the position of the wind flags, call the shot, and you've gained valuable insight. An added advantage is, calling shots increases the level of concentration achieved during the string. Continue using this valuable tool during practice and matches, it keeps you sharp and on your toes.

Informal practice sessions where you shoot non match-grade components doesn't do anything but burn up the barrel. I've seen shooters who shoot Nosler or Sierra match bullets in practice. Thinking they're saving money is the reason I've heard. It's foolish to practice with anything but the best available. Others use an old 6x47 or .222 for practice saying they're saving their "match" gun for competition. I can guarantee the guys who win the next match have set up top of the line equipment and components for practice. Pay the piper one way or the other: buy another good barrel for your good rifle, or use an accurate practice rifle, but shoot the best you've got. In the 1940's and 1950's it was lots harder for a shooter to get his equipment into top form. He had to struggle to get a barrel that shot the way any one of our current match grade barrels do. Back then it might have made sense to "save" the one good barrel, it had a much shorter accuracy life than current barrels, that tube might not have been replaceable.

### Pick a Condition

I like to have an idea of which condition I'll shoot before arriving at the line. Watch the flags and verify the condition is still around while setting up the rests and waiting for commence fire. Check the mirage and make sure it's following the actions of the flags you're watching. Tony Boyer has a common house key, mounted on a pivot, on the front of his case block. To decrease the possibility of confusion Tony flips the key in the direction of the mirage when he starts a string. If your condition has been staying long enough, or is coming back quickly, test with at least two shots on the sighter at the beginning of the relay. If the fouler and sighter are exactly where you expect them, if the wind up range is showing the same steady flow, go ahead, start the group and run off as many shots as possible. At 100 yards and in great conditions at 200 yards I always look for a condition that gets two shots touching on the sighter. The only time I cut out the two shot touching rule is when the conditions have been snotty all day and big groups are the norm. Then, if the range officer says commence fire just as a calm settles in I'll fire one fouler to see where the group will impact in the calm and go immediately to the record target. That first record shot is in essence another sighter since you can see if it hits where the fouler landed. If the placement is ok I'll run my fastest string and try to finish before the wind picks up. Sometimes this is the way to steal the smallest group of the day. If that first record shot was off in outer space, stop, check on the sighter and try to hold the group together with some picking and running in the bad conditions. It's worth a try to get a good group off in that brief calm. If the days conditions are really rough you probably didn't hurt yourself too badly.

On a normal day if the first two sighter shots didn't touch or if one of them stepped out, against what the flags told you to expect, there's still plenty of time to pick and choose a good group. The smallest groups come when you don't have to hold very far. If the first shot is on the bottom of the

*Notice the competitors concentration during set-up. Irene Fazio, Dennis Wagner, and Rex Reneau study the conditions.*

moth ball and the sighter shows the new condition needs two bullets of hold over it's easy to end up with a group in the .3s or .4s rather than a .1. It takes experience to find the days best condition, but, THE MOST IMPORTANT THING FOR SMALL GROUPS IS STARTING IN THE RIGHT CONDITION.

In decent conditions don't force the first or second shot if there's plenty of time. We can all shoot five shots in a minute or minute and a half. Why shoot a big group in the first two minutes of a relay and leave five minutes for sitting at the bench and looking at the mess you made out of your target. When that happens it usually means the last three minutes of the relay will be the best calm of the day.

While you're practicing or at a shoot be observant. Once in a while orient your focus outside the loading bench. In Kelbly's big barn I like to get up in the middle of the reloading process and step outside to see if the wind tendency's changed in the few minutes since the end of the relay. When it's an outside reloading area, if you're out of sight of the range flags, you can always observe trees, grass, and debris as the conditions stir them.

By keeping track of general trends it's much easier to adapt next time you shoot. If you know the wind is changing over from left to right after being the other way all morning it's easy to be confident and start a group in this new condition. Any time you're at the range for a practice session set up flags and wind a stop watch; run practice just like a real match. Fire a fouler, test the dominant conditions early, use the sighter and flags for real. Find out which ones aren't lying to you. Watch a flag 20 yards out. Does the shot move further out during a pick up? Does it come back into the group as it lets up? Test angle changes on the head winds. Does a shot move into the wind when comparing a 9 o'clock breeze with an 11 o'clock head wind that's stronger? How about vertical from that 11 o'clock head wind? Did you know that with direction being constant, the only change in intensity, angled heavy breezes working on the rotation of the bullet can give you a 45 degree slot: it's similar to Nolan Ryan throwing a curve ball. If you test that new zinger without flags, what have you learned, nothing happens except burning powder, hurting the dirt in the backstop, and shortening the life of the barrel.

If the 20 yard flag isn't consistent look further out. This is a perfect time to find the flag that's showing the bullet deflection. When a shot steps out, after that 20 yard flag said it should drop into the group, immediately look down range and find the flag that explains the movement. Is there some special piece of topography you've missed that's letting an uninhibited breeze influence the shot? Unless the Virginia gang puts up their 20 foot tall wind flags Mainville is much tougher to shoot on the right side with its big hole. Painted Post has only a few places to put wind flags close to the bullet path, it looks like a moto cross track with berms, jumps, and water (sometimes they use a motorcycle to change targets). Council Cup can influence shots meaningfully after 100 yards. They have an open area where the wind whistles down and moves the bullet more than you would think. Midland in a blow can be one tough mother. Take a walk down range sometime and look at the clear shot the wind has at your bullet. Howard Dietz's New Braunfels range, Central Jersey, and Kelbly's all have significant man made structures that change the wind patterns. If you're lucky enough to test on the same range where you will compete it's a big advantage.

Get used to measuring and recording every practice group. If you've never measured groups before it's a simple thing. First you need an accurate dial, or vernier, caliper. Rest the target on a flat surface where there's plenty of light. Glance at the target and decide which line presents the widest distance between shots; if the group is a triangle where both dimensions look the same you'll have to measure both directions. Rotate the target so the group runs left to right, open the caliper and carefully place the left handed jaw so it's exactly touching the outside black of the left hand bullet hole. Press down on the left hand jaw so it doesn't move while you gingerly open the right hand jaw till it exactly touches the outside of the black of the right hand bullet hole. Lift the caliper and read the measurement to the nearest .001″. Since we're looking for the distance between the center-to-center of the widest shots, subtract one bullet diameter from that measurement. For example: a 6mm group which measures .467″ outside-to-outside

*If you're ever going to shoot a group in the zeroes this is the time. A barely moving flag tells you to shoot a good one.*

gives a final measurement of .467″ - .243″, or .224″. A nice group at 100 yards.

Become familiar with the different pitfalls that await you during a match. Work out what to do if the common ones occur. A bullet stuck in the throat when you try to remove a live round can be knocked out with a cleaning rod. Same goes for a fired case in the chamber with a weak extractor. Be careful with both of those situations, the powder that falls out of a full case usually puts the rifle out of commission. Jef Fowler keeps a rifle patched out, with loaded rounds ready, behind the line at big matches. A case neck that pulls off in the chamber puts the rifle out of commission in a hurry. Use a clean, tight, brush on the end of a cleaning rod to remove the separated neck. Insert the brush with a twisting motion, slowly twist it in - then out, to catch and remove the neck. Sticking the brush straight in - then out of the chamber jams the brush if the bristles go as far as the rifling. Since brushes are set up with oversize bristles to get better leverage on deposits they are bent over slightly when they get to the bore section. Sticking the brush straight into the chamber at the least can become frustrating, and at the worst might cause things to become airborne (now who would throw anything just because the range master just said "one minute").

If you insert the primers backwards, leave them or powder out, seven minutes is plenty of time to run back, reload a few rounds and finish the group. Boy, do the components fly when that happens. When there are only a few minutes left and you find a row without powder or primer, there isn't time to trot back to the loading area, ask a shooter who has finished to loan you their rifle to complete the group.

The most important thing practice gives is familiarity with wind flags, sighter shots, and conditions. I'll repeat this over and over again throughout the book. When the shot steps out, look immediately and find the flag which shows that movement. Make excuses after losing shots and you'll never catch up to the hot shooters. Speaking of hot shooters, no matter how good you are, this is a sport of individuals. Be humble, be a good sport. Know the rulebook and look for opportunities to give a struggling competitor any help allowed within the rules. There's been ten or twelve times I've loaned a rifle for someone to finish a group, and many more times I helped spot shots for someone encountering trouble getting on target after a scope or barrel change. Be aware of those around you and help make someone's weekend. In all my several hundred matches I've only once run into totally uncalled for unsportsmanship. Marge Masker and I were mingling with a group at the end of a days shooting, during the 1985 IBS Nationals, when a competitor I nipped in the 2-Gun charged up and put his foot deep inside his mouth with a ridiculous statement. When winning becomes so important common sense and decency go out the window, something of great value in the sport has been lost. Go out of your way to keep your conduct in line with the rules of good sportsmanship.

The difference between a fun shooter and a champion can be great. The fun shooter can have most of the basics of equipment and style down, but it is consistent application of the fundamentals which makes the champion. The champion will be a diligent student of the sport. They study the things which make small groups, and aggregates, then practice till they are ingrained. Equipment is tested and scrutinized till it's as perfect as they can get it. Any match in a reasonable distance, and some which aren't, gets attended. There's no free ride, hard work is the only way to get to the top. It's a tough challenge but any shooter with enough desire can climb to the pinnacle.

# 13

# *Light Varmint*

Arriving at a weekend's 2-gun match with only a light rifle creates no disadvantage for the competitive shooter who has his technique down and can hold a light rifle the same for every shot. Correctly made 10 1/2 pound Light Varmint or Sporter rifles will shoot to the same level as a 13 1/2 pound Heavy Varmint, there should be absolutely no difference in the accuracy potential between the two. Because of the small powder charges burned by the current 6mm benchrest wildcats a 10 1/2 pound rifle, shooting a 68 grain bullet at 3300 fps, has a recoil of only five foot pounds. With a shoulder thump substantially less than any of the normal hunting calibers a shooter can remove his hold as a possible source of error. You can "free recoil" these light rifles and not pound yourself silly over the course of a weekend. Bruising was the case in the days before the PPC when shooters like Jim Stekl and Bob White used 10 1/2 pound .308s for all three classes in a weekends Light Varmint, Sporter, Heavy Varmint 3-Gun aggregate. For years I've shot the skeletized CPS aluminum stock free recoil. The only range where recoil became a problem was in Mainville, Pennsylvania. Mainville uses the best of all bullet traps, a mountain. Only problem is; because of a lack of flat areas the range is build on a slope. The 300 yard target butts are on an incline over 90 feet above the shooting bench. Rifles aimed at a target that far above them get a little help from gravity when they recoil from a shot. That little 1/2" wide butt stock on the Light Varmint raises a bruise when it gets that kind of a running start. Whenever I shot a return-to-battery gun at Mainville it tried to recoil into my lap on every shot.

The typical light rifle can be made of the same components used to make up a Heavy Varmint. There are different versions of stocks, actions, and barrels which are made a little smaller to weigh less for the 10 1/2 pound classes. Since the advent of fibreglass stocks, internally adjusted scopes, and light weight actions much of the penalty for the three pound difference between Heavy and Light Varmint has disappeared. There are two main schools of thought about how to produce a competitive light rifle: some gunsmiths think longer barrel length, and the velocity it produces, is the secret to make a competitive light rifle. They'll use a slimmer tube and make the barrel 23"-24". The other school of thought is to use the maximum allowable dimensioned "max heavy" Heavy Varmint barrel and shorten it to make weight. These gunsmiths believe the way to good groups is through the stiffness of a heavier barrel. Belonging to the group who believe stiffness gives more than length takes away, light rifles in my gun chest use max heavy barrels in the 20 1/2" length. Threaded into a light weight aluminum/steel action like the MCS or Stolle, dropped into one of the featherweight Kevlar or graphite stocks, topped by an internally adjusted target scope like the Leupold 36X, these stout barrels make weight without any problem. Proof is in the pudding as they say. In the instance of choosing and shooting a competitive light rifle the pudding could be anything from pistachio to banana cream. There have been multitudes of rifles built, either longer and more slender, or shorter and fatter, which have been winners.

The original Hart Stainless Steel barrel for my I-beam Light Varmint was a prize from the 1981 Super Shoot. 106th place in Heavy Varmint just happened to be the lucky position. After seeing the quality of the prize for 106th I stopped complaining about shooting four groups in the threes and one group of .807" at 100 yards. Neither will there be any angry remarks about the barrels performance: shooting it as a 6PPC in both Varmint classes for the next year and a half it totaled 33 Grand Aggregates. The last week-end the barrel fired with that chamber was a Heavy Varmint Light Varmint match at Camillus, New York. Six out of the 12 five- shot groups at 100 yards were below .250", small group was .142". At 200 yards five of the 12 groups were below .500", small group was .355". The bore had seen innumerable rounds, it looked like an alligator for the first several inches. There was so much copper attaching to the bad section: patches coming out of the barrel when it was time to go back to the line were bright lime green.

That year Al Shipman had travelled over from Germany to get some practical experience in benchrest and shoot in a couple matches, he dragged Wally Hart to Camillus, they were loading together next tent over from me. I took those green patches to Wally and asked his opinion. He said "If they are showing that much green and the rifle is shooting so well it must mean the solvent is getting out most of the copper". Even with 4000+ rounds through the barrel it buried a 1.362" 200 yard mistake (saying it was a mistake is being polite) and won the 2-gun with a .2707 2-Gun Aggregate. Mike Toth cut off two inches and put in a new chamber. At 18 1/2" it will still win any match where I read the conditions and point shots in the right direction. Chronograph testing this barrel at the shorter length shows a 62.5

*Another time a nice guy finished first, Phil Sauer shows off the 1982 IBS Three-Gun trophy.*

grain bullet in front of 27.8 grains of H322, in a blown out .220 Russian case, achieves 3150 fps.

Several shooters believe familiarity and consistency build winning scores. Most of us can't spend the time to get several rifles to the peak of their form for every match. It's easier to have one rifle to focus on; without a division of effort the end product is better. In IBS matches where both 100 yard Aggregates are shot on Saturday, and both 200 yard Aggregates are shot on Sunday, using only one rifle puts you in top form for the afternoon shooting. Point of impact is exactly where you want it- there's no adjusting the scope, then going right into the match - understanding of wind and mirage effect on that exact combination puts us in top form from the very first match in the afternoon. By restricting ourselves to only one rifle the cost of competing is pared significantly. Only one new barrel gets fitted at the beginning of the season. No need for several scopes to gather dust while they sit in the gun cabinet. There is a famous old saying: "It's better to wear out than rust out". Never is this more true than in benchrest. Unless we're fortunate and shoot every weekend there's not at all enough time spent with the rifles in the rack to become completely familiar with all of them. Some of the best tack drivers I've seen were ones someone tired of. New shooters picked up these "throw downs" for much less than the cost of new, and proceeded to whip the old owner as soon as they learned to dance with the wind. In Houston one of the best ways to buy a shooter for less than full price is to purchase a used benchrest rifle from Richard Warwick: they were originally built with the best components, they haven't seen enough wear to be tired, and they all shoot like a house afire. I bought an old black rifle in 6PPC from Ed Joiner a few years ago at the Super Shoot. It wasn't fancy: glass stock, Hart Barrel, and 2 oz. trigger, on an accurized 40X sleeved action. Dr. John Stafford of Houston got it from me for something on the order of $500. It took him half a year or so to realize the wind was pushing the bullet while it made its brief sprint for freedom. Then he thumped everyone at a Lake Charles, Louisiana Heavy Varmint match with a 100 yard range aggregate in the .1's. As is usually the case, his first gloating words after jumping up and down were: "You want to buy it back?"

For a new shooter interested in benchrest I strongly suggest they enter the game through the used equipment route. It takes anywhere from one to two years of shooting before a new benchrest shooters ability is up to the capability of a brand new benchrest rifle. By purchasing a used rifle the new participant gets free use of a rifle over that learning period. When they think it's time for a new rig that used gun can be sold for almost as much as when it was purchased, better yet; put on a new barrel. Since there's a large chunk of change in the rest of the equipment needed (like rests, bags, flags, and loading tools) buying used to begin with spreads the investment out over a few years. Buying that first gun as a Light Varmint lets you get twice as much shooting for half the cost.

I believe that anytime I go to the line with a light rifle there is a definite chance to win either of the Varmint aggregates. For the first three years of competition finances were such there was never enough money for a second 36X scope. I had that old 6BR for Heavy Varmint and the I- Beam 6PPC for Light Varmint. The first few matches in 1982 I would set up the 6BR with the scope, shoot the mornings Heavy Varmint aggregate, switch the scope over to the light rifle in the afternoon, and shoot the afternoons aggregate. In the evening the scope was put back on the 13 1/2 pounder for the next morning. It was the scope switch for the 200 yard afternoon match which got exciting. The mirage would be boiling, combined with wind movement the sighter target rings would jump and dance, the range targets we're supposed to use to sight in on have lots of holes in them by then so it's impossible to tell which are yours. Sometimes on days with bad mirage you can't even see the holes at 200 yards. After a few scares, having problems getting sighted in at 200 yards, I stopped switching scopes and rifles. The 6BR went back in the closet; the light rifle shot both aggregates.

Ranges typically run a few minutes behind after the mornings event. If there are only two relays and the range crew decides to start the afternoons event immediately after the finish of the mornings aggregate you go crazy trying to clean the mornings gun, get out the loading tools for the different case, load up some new rounds, clean the afternoons gun, switch scopes,

*Faye Boyer: one of the toughest competitors in benchrest.*

and get to the line on time. I've seen people who dropped out of the afternoon's event because they couldn't get ready in time.

The smallest groups I've ever fired at 100 and 200 yards have been shot with a light rifle. Two years in a row I fired the smallest 100 yard group at the IBS Nationals. A .080″ in 1981, and an .093″ in 1982. The smallest group I've ever fired in competition was at the 1985 Super Shoot. The I-Beam put a .074″ downrange, it came within .001″ of being small group of the match. One of the Italian visitors shot a .073″ to take home the gorgeous coaster set for small group at 100 yards. 1985 was also the year for my smallest 200 yard group. I've already related the story of shooting the last two shots in a reverse to hold together a .134″ five shot group. When the dot in the target stays as small as that after several shots I'm glad a doctor isn't taking my blood pressure and pulse. Surely they would both be off the top of the scale.

Several times competitive shooters have used their 10 1/2 pound rifles for all three, or all four classes at the Nationals. Bob Adamowicz of Holden, Massachusetts, creator of the XPISMS system (XP100 integral scope mounting system, a machined device with the sleeve, and rings all out of one piece of aluminum, mated to a Kevlar stock) used his 10 1/2 pound 6PPC to win the IBS Heavy Varmint, Light Varmint, Heavy Bench 3-Gun Aggregate in 1984. Friend, and always tough competitor Turk Takano used his varmint rifle the same way. His statement was: "This is a really good barrel, it will shoot as well as anything else I could have brought, on ten shot groups it's very fast." Whichever method you use to make a light rifle keep it in balance. When a rifle gets nose heavy, it moves inconsistently on recoil and group size suffers. With the I-Beam CPS and its light skeletized butt this is especially important. Bob White had to resort to downwards thumb pressure on the bar behind the trigger to get his to shoot. I've been lucky, never had to put any external pressure on mine to get good groups out of it. Check the rifle with a sensitive scale to find out where the center of gravity will be. The barrel of a light rifle will weigh four or five pounds. If it's too far forward of the front rest support point accuracy will degrade. If the rifle is nose heavy try different bag positions, see if moving the front rest forward brings down the size of the groups.

Shooters struggling to make weight on certified scales lead to some of the best antics of the weekend. Benchrest gunsmiths keep accurate scales in the shop to make sure the rifle will make weight before it goes out the door. It's the changing of components which gets you in trouble. My Light Varmint rifle weighs exactly ten pounds seven ounces. The addition of a sheet of paper for a mirage shield moves the weight into the one ounce allowable variation. If the rifle was set up with light weight rings and no butt plate the changeover to heavier rings or the addition of a rubber butt plate would put most rifles over the limit. If it's the first time the rifle has been weighed on certified scales there are a few things to remove to try and make weight. Most obvious is to check and see if the bore guide is still in the action! I've seen people rip apart their rifle when it was just an extra piece putting them over weight. Then one at a time remove the scope caps, scope mirage shield, scope sun shield, and the scope adjusting knobs. If you still haven't made weight, but are close, try taking off the trigger guard and the bolt stop if it comes out. One of the older heavier Lyman scopes could be switched over to a Leupold 36X, or the lighter 24X. Anything else is more drastic. If that still hasn't done it and you really want to shoot get out a hack saw and remove an inch from the butt stock. Hacksaw blades don't do anything but work up a sweat if the stock is made of Kevlar. There's a true story from the days of wood stocks where a famous shooter came to a match with a new rifle which didn't make weight. He got out a hatchet and proceeded to chop off the cheek piece! Before going to such drastic means as the hacksaw try borrowing a spare gun from someone on the line. Get the range officer to explain the predicament over the loud speaker, there's sure to be someone who will help.

If there are any complaints about shooting one light rifle in both classes it would have to be fouling buildup and case stickiness by the end of 24 matches. Pushing 68 grain bullets as fast as we do it's only a matter of time before the barrel starts to build up copper fouling. Solvent only gets half an hour to act on the copper before we patch out and spin more bullets down the tube. When shooting the rifle in one class there are only five or six groups before it gets a major cleaning at night and again the next day.

Solvent sitting overnight should remove most of the built up copper fouling. If the rifle is used in both classes the time in use goes up to ten or twelve groups before the major cleaning. By the end of the weekend it would have to be a good barrel not to foul with copper. The second problem is also from hot loads. Depending on shooter preference, and their aversion to tight cases, 24 firings before resizing might be too long. I've never had a problem shooting the same cases several weekends between resizings. The load I use seems to get the cases, and the bolt, to a certain level of effort (stickiness) and then gets no tighter. Again, it all depends on the load you use, the pressure it develops, and whether hard closing bolts bother you.

The Sporter class has outlived its usefulness in its present form. Originally the Sporter Class was developed to get the serious shooter working bullets larger than .224", and the case designs to shoot it accurately. The standard rifle in the 10 1/2 pound classes is the same for both Light Varmint (where any caliber is permissible) and Sporter (where the bullet must be .243" or larger). As of this writing there have been several serious attempts to get the Sporter class rules amended so the class is back to its initial purpose. That is - the breeding of experimental rifles and case designs. Otherwise nice guys have shot down any attempt at a change of the rules whenever it's been on the years agenda. They've been so adamant as to get moratoriums placed so no rule changes can be submitted for the next several years!

The Sporter class needs to carry on its tradition as a test bed for the other classes. A few suggestions for what to do with the class seem to make sense, a few aren't as valid. Most of the proposals have been in the areas of weight or caliber restrictions. I'm not happy with the advocates of the weight restriction change. I've seen several sample which incorporated all the lightweight technology available; one weighed less than six pounds with a scope. Using a light weight stock, aluminum/steel action, and fluted barrel there wouldn't be any need for experimentation, we would have created a light-Light Varmint class with no change in technology required.

The change which makes the most sense is to go to a larger caliber. Originally, in the Sporter class it was difficult to shoot good targets. Bullets were the out of the box type from a couple of the big manufacturers. For many years the only case which had any success was the finicky 6X47. It took many years for Sporter class rifles to achieve any respect. With the advent of the 6PPC the only rifle most shooters use in the 10 1/2 pound classes is a Sporter. Now it's time to take another giant step forward. Let's do the right thing for our sport and make the minimum caliber for Sporter class .257". Bring back the experimentation!

Created in 1960, at the insistence of Col. Townsend Whelen, the Light Varmint and Heavy Varmint classes have steadily increased in popularity till they've taken over the role of top dog in benchrest competition.

# 14

# *Heavy Varmint*

Heavy Varmint, the most popular class, is the backbone of competitive benchrest shooting. The 1988 Super Shoot, with almost 280 entrants in Heavy Varmint, was held over the Memorial Day weekend at George Kelbly's North Lawrence, Ohio range. Being centrally located the Super Shoot is usually the best attended of the years major matches. Warren Page stated back in 1972 that the current rifles, and the shooters behind them, weren't capable of 1/4 minute of angle aggregates over the 100 and 200 yard course of fire. (This means averaging .250″ for five groups at 100 yards and averaging .500″ for five groups at 200 yards.) We've made great strides since 1972 - both in equipment and in shooting ability. The Super Shoot is an exciting event since it gets a great majority of the countries notable shooters together in shoulder to shoulder competition. If you do well at a match this important you deserve to be proud.

At the 1988 Super Shoot Joe Kabel had his shooting stick rounded into shape in the 100 yard Heavy Varmint aggregate. He shot a .336″ group in the warm-up, it was good for a 139th place tie. Joe's first record match was a .254″ group, that gave him 63rd place. The second record was a nice .142″ effort, it gave him fourth place for that match. The third record group was a .192″, another fine group giving a tie for 20th. The fourth record group yielded a .269″ score, good for a 65th place tie. The final record group measured .249″ and a tie for 41st. Looking at these scores, all shot in windy conditions, we see the formula for a winning effort. Joe shot his biggest group of the day on the warm-up, so it gets thrown away. On this windy day every group stayed below .300″, then he threw in two targets in the .1's to lower the aggregate to .2212. Compare this score to the figure for Joe Bernard, one of my favorite Canadians (have Joe tell you the joke about the guy who had his arm replaced). His scores were .499″ on the warm-up, then

*Jeff Stover sets up a 10 1/2 pounder for a Heavy Varmint match. Well done light rifles shoot every bit as well as the heavier rifles.*

.421", .323", .431", .236", and .199". Joe's worst placing on any record match was 207th for his .421 on the first match (this means his .421" beat over 70 shooters, you know the day was windy). His best placing was 15th for the .199. Remember, these groups were shot in tough, windy, conditions - the two groups in the fours were well below what some people were struggling with. Again, the two small groups pulled the aggregate down to a respectable .3220 moa effort and 90th place overall, still in the top third.

Kelbly's range has 60 benches: with a line that long there are lots of wind flags spread out to give a real good indication of wind patterns, with 280 shooters broken up into five relays there are always a few who get a little calm to lay down for them while running a string, and catch a good group. That day my small group at 100 yards was a .136" on the fourth record, it only netted fifth place for the match. Small groups appear at every well attended match, even when it's generally snotty. The match winning scores for 100 yards were Larry Baggetts .125" for the warm-up, the first record Bob Broyles shot a .085" group (Brad Rosenthal was second with a .086", sometimes it's just not your day) new shooter Kit Jansen decided to make her presence felt, she won the second record with a .113" group, Fred Sinclair shot a .113" to win the third record, Paul Mitchell was the victor in the fourth with a .111" cluster, and Michael Haines cracked the "zeroes" with an .097" for the fifth record. Every one of these groups created a 5-shot hole in the paper not much larger than a standard pencil eraser, a dime easily covers any of them with lots of room to spare. On a windy day it's a tribute to the skill level of todays marksman that these tiny groups still appear. For the largest match winner to be Larry's .125″ makes a significant statement. One tiny group could be a fluke, which is the way the old timers of the 40's, 50's, 60's, and early 70's spoke about little groups like these. The day is here when a big event like the Super Shoot requires a group approaching the "zeroes" to be a match winner.

In a Grand Aggregate the 100 yard competition is often considered the warm-up, you want to stay close to the leaders, but you don't need to be in first place. 200 yards is the true test of the competent shooter and the 200 yard conditions the next day were easier to figure out. Lowell Frei of St. George, Utah shot 200 yard groups of .563″, .547″, .433″, .438″, and .478″ for an admirable 200 yard aggregate of .2459 moa. When added to his second place from 100 yards Lowell had a Grand Aggregate of .2336 moa. It seems the day Warren Page knew was in the future has arrived, not only has the 1/4 minute of angle rifle and the 1/4 minute of angle rifleman truly arrived, several people have stayed under .2500 for a 2-Gun aggregate!

Let's compare Lowells scores with another Canadian. Paul Burns shot a .3856 aggregate that day for 85th place at 200 yards. You know the conditions were laying down a little bit when you see his .792″ group on the warm-up was only good for 189th place. The record string included groups of .475″, .755″, .893″, 1.014″ and .719″. His .474″ target was good for 21st place, the 1.014″ target was 148th place. Another good example of the need for perseverance, don't quit after shooting a group over an inch at 200 yards, the conditions are undoubtedly rougher than earlier in the morning, everyone else is having a tougher time also. Pauls .719″ target in the fifth match helped keep his placing in the top third for the 200 yard Range Aggregate. To win a match trophy that day you had to stay in the "twos". Howy Levy won the warm-up with a .204″, John Eaton won the first record with a .222″, Dennis Wagner won the second with a .232″, Tom Peria was in on the third with a .214″, Rex Reneau got the fourth with a .258″ (Come on Rex, you shot the biggest match winner, you'll have to try harder next year) and the fifth match went to Merlin Hubbard with a tidy .238″. Just like the 100 yard match winners we see the same story. All of these 200 yard groups would be completely covered by a dime!

The 13 1/2 pound weight limit in the Heavy Varmint class lets the shooter build just about any configuration and style allowable in the rules. There are a few generalities in the top of the line Heavy Varmint rifle's components. All use a stainless steel match grade barrel, all use synthetic stocks (Bob DeMonstoy - a lumber mill operator - for several years shot a wood stock with a bumper sticker on it saying: "Wood Is Beautiful", last I saw even he had switched over to synthetic) all will use a two ounce trigger, 80% have a custom single shot action, and all will be topped with a high power scope somewhere between 25 and 40 power (with an 80% preference for the 36

*The big matches get most of the countries top shooters together in shoulder to shoulder competition. Unlike other sports; rookies can compete in the nationals.*

power). In the 1987 Crawfish Invitational at Lafayette, Louisiana only one of the top 20 Heavy Varmint finishers used a modified commercial action (the commercial actions used in the Varmint classes include the Remington 40X, XP100, 600, and 700) only one used a scope of less than 30 power. In the 1987 Super Shoot's top 20 there were four modified commercial actions, but only one scope below 36 power.

Using an aluminum/steel two inch wide CPS action with an R&M Precision Kevlar stock and 24″ Hart stainless steel max heavy barrel I still had to add a pound and a half of lead in the buttstock to get up to the weight limit. Shooters from the 60's and 70's had to worry about the weight of the wood stock and the weight of the heavy scopes then available. We're lucky now: without the struggle to shave ounces it's easy to get a Heavy Varmint to shoot well.

In the Light Varmint class we made a decision whether we wanted a skinny and long barrel or a fat and short barrel. In the Heavy Varmint class we don't have to make that decision, synthetic stocks allow us to go fat and long on the tube. A "max heavy" barrel (made to the maximum allowable dimensions) can still be 22″ to 24″ without going over the weight limit. The Heavy Varmints extra three pounds of rifle weight gets recoil down around four foot pounds for a normal load. Four foot pounds is light enough that all but the frailest can shoot free-recoil without bruising. When you're trying to get your wife interested in shooting start her off with the Heavy Varmint and its light recoil; it's a lot easier convincing someone they're having fun when they aren't getting socked on every shot.

If you've never had a custom gun built and can afford to buy new look over the line at a benchrest match, check out some of the rifles, ask questions about various shooters likes and dislikes, write up a list of the components you think will make up the perfect rifle for you, show the list to a few of the competitors for their suggestions, then go ahead and order a custom rig.

For the gunner whose only interest is in shooting for fun at his range on weekends, and participating in one or two local matches over the year, the Heavy Varmint is the best choice. It's slightly easier to shoot the heavier rifle. A little more forgiving, they ride the bags better, and are steadier than 10 1/2 pounders. By being more charitable the heavier rifles achieve better groups for the shooter whose technique is still a little ragged. For some recoil sensitive shooters the heavier rifle helps the flinch a bit. My friend Jim Williams works here in Houston at a local sporting goods dealer with a rifle range attached. He gets to step out his door, walk 10 paces, and he has a place to shoot. The problem is, the dealer offers a service to hunting types who need their big boomers sighted in. Jim is forced to sight-in lots of rifles, including hundreds of big magnums all the way up to bruisers like the .378 Weatherby, over the course of the season. Elmer Keith would have loved it, but a skinny guy like Jim takes such a pounding it becomes hard to exorcise the flinch later in the year - even with light recoiling PPCs. For Jim the three pound difference helps him shoot better in Heavy Varmint.

# 15

# *Unlimited/Heavy Bench*

Heavy Bench is the foundation on which competitive benchrest was built; until the institution of the Varmint classes in 1960 Heavy Bench was the only game in town. The big gun that our fore-fathers cut their teeth on in the sports first decade and a half was likely an 18 pound, slab of wood stocked, Mauser 98 action rebarreled to a wildcat Gregoire barrel. The .219 Donaldson was the cartridge of preference when stuffed with hand made bullets, or the accurate pills from several of the manufacturers. Those wood stocks were one of the limiting factors in the accuracy potential in the rifle. Todays glue-ins all but eliminate grouping problems caused by bedding. The Mauser 98 and its contemporaries had such a small bedding area the rifleman who wanted the best performance was required to re-bed before every match, and sometimes overnight between classes! Gale McMillan stated it's a shame the old days are gone. He said, because of the new stocks and their removal of the bedding problem you don't have to be as competent to be a good shooter or a benchrest gunsmith anymore.

I couldn't disagree more strongly. The best days of benchrest are now, and the revitalized Heavy Bench class is helping lead the way. The original purpose of shooting groups was to test new ideas and get the best accuracy out of the equipment. It states right in the IBS rule book, the purpose of the organization is: "The development and encouragement of uniform competition to achieve extreme accuracy in firearms, ammunition, equipment, and shooting methods". The NBRSA rule book has a similar statement. It's in Heavy Bench where most of the experimenting is going on today.

I don't agree with all the developments from the last few years, but we won't know where the outside limit of rifle accuracy is if we place artificial constraints on the allowable equipment. Crawford Hollidge wrote a benchrest article in 1962 bemoaning the fact they were allowing mechan-

*The late Nate Boop shot a 300 yard 10 shot group of .675" with a 10 1/2 pound rifle! Now that's what I call shooting.*

ical rests in the class. He thought the gadgets were "ruining" benchrest. Some things never change. An example to point out why we want a class without restraints is to look at what happened to the 12 Meter sailboats. They, along with a lot of the other racing sailboat classes, have been developed to where the boats try to be rule beaters rather than the best sailboats. Every sport needs a class where there are no outside limits, otherwise there's no future; only stagnation.

Heavy Bench guns fire 10 shot groups in a 12 minute time span. Ten shot groups at 200 yards can be one of the most frustrating moments you'll ever run into. With a little mirage and some switching wind it wouldn't matter if you had all day, the tight little group is elusive. It's happened several times where I wanted to stop a group after seven or eight shots. The existing hole would be in the "zeroes", and you know the last shots to finish the record group would obliterate the tiny hole.

There are several styles of rifle used in the Heavy Bench class. The first would be the varmint weight rifle with a varmint sized barrel that's fired because the owner doesn't have a heavy gun and wants to participate (the so called "Rat Gun"). There have been a few surprises over the years when the light gun shooter got hot and pasted all the big boys to the wailing wall.

The second style of Heavy Bench gun is one Dave Brennan popularized several years ago. It's called "cruiser" weight. Take a Heavy Varmint, chamber up a straight taper 1.250" barrel and shoot it off bags like a big

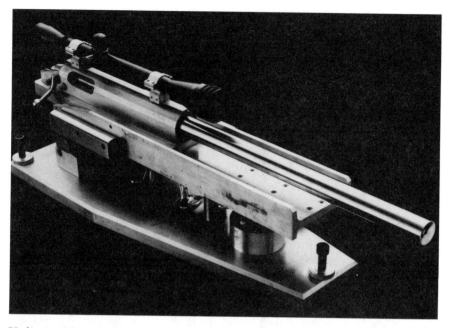

*Unlimited benchrest rifles are the ultimate for tack driving accuracy. Rail guns return to the same aiming point after every shot.*

varmint gun. It can really get to work on the days where mirage and quick switches screw the return-to-battery shooters into the ground. The straight barrel easily handles the extra heat from ten shot groups and a few extra sighters. Seely Masker's shot a fat barrel on his 40X for years. I was a referee one weekend when he got hot, and signed a 100 yard group he was submitting for official record measurement. As I recall it was a ten shot group in the order of .129″. One benefit from shooting a cruiser is its speed during switching conditions. With a sloped buttstock sighter shots are quick, then movement back to the record happens before the condition switches again. The biggest advantage I can see for this style rifle is for the older, smaller, or physically challenged shooter. Since the rifle weighs half what a full big gun weighs it's easier to man-handle over the course of the weekend. I remember Homer Culver, a great Heavy Bench shooter, comment at the end of a long weekend he was never going to haul his thirty-five pounder around again.

The next step up in equipment is to a true "big gun". It will be purpose built for the Heavy Bench class. The average weight for this style is in the 30-35 pound range. The butt will ride on a flat rear sandbag, typically there will be a rod set into the flat bottomed butt, the bar creases into the rear sandbag and provides some measure of guidance and tracking, yet still easily deflects to hold off quickly in switching conditions. The fore end is also wider than on the varmint rifles, inletted steel bars ride on a synthetic or wood plate attached to the normal front pedestal top. A groove in the plate, or any of a number of variations, gives positive lateral support and straight tracking on recoil and return to battery. These rifles are great when there's no mirage running and quick changes in aim are required. The full return to battery guns thump them easily when there's enough mirage the shooter doesn't get an accurate resight after a shot. My biggest complaint with this style of rifle is their lack of cams to go between record and sighter target easily and quickly. The one I shoot has to be moved from record to sighter and back again with the screw threads of the star-wheel on the front pedestal. It's much too slow to use the sighter target effectively in switching conditions.

The last style is the true "Unlimited" rifle. It's another purpose built gun. Usually on a machined slab of I-beam, sometimes with two piece mechanical rests, sometimes with one piece mechanical rests these "iron monsters" have given this sport most of it's recent experimentation. Several years ago the class rules were changed making one piece mechanical rests legal. There has been a surge in interest in the full return-to-battery rifle because of these rule changes. With full return to battery capability the competitor isn't screwed by mirage effect on the sight picture. Where the bag gun shooter must resight after every shot the rail-gun shooter throws the rig forward to its stop, reloads and touches the trigger for another perfectly aimed shot. Rail- guns can be reloaded and fired quickly. Ten shot strings in 35 seconds are easy. Turk Takano can get all ten off in 25 seconds. That's so fast the moving backer might not register all the shots at 100 yards, subsequent bullets with a little left or right drift can double into previous holes and cut a slot, resulting in disqualification if all the shots aren't visible. The advantages of return-to-battery go out the window when the conditions won't stay the same for any two shots. With the flags switching like crazy is when the bag shooter cleans up.

Average weight for the competitive big guns run in the 30- 40 pound range without rests. The rests can easily double the weight of the rig, the old Ferguson front rest was over 25 pounds all by itself. Bob Adamowicz of Holden Massachusetts shot a big gun with a weight system that brought overall weight up to 125 pounds. The extra weight didn't make it perform any better, in fact it shot better in the 50 pound range. The PPC and its contemporaries develop only a few pounds of recoil, with my thirty one pounder the rifle only moves six or seven inches after a shot. At a match where we have to rotate to a new bench after every target anything over 50 pounds is too heavy to lug between benches. Any rifle that weighs 40 or 50 pounds should have a pull-along golf cart to move them from the car to the bench, or between benches.

Several gunsmiths and small manufacturers started producing complete, ready to shoot, unlimited rifles with one piece rests. The Hall Unlimited Rifle, by Bill Hall is the gun with widespread use. For a reasonable price, considering the amount of work in one, a shooter can have an unlimited big gun that is absolutely the top of the line for rifle accuracy. That's a heady thought, there will be no rifles in the entire world with better accuracy, only some which are its equal. The prettiest rig is the set-up John Jones of Friendswood, Texas builds. A massive affair machined out of aluminum, John has built one of the most accurate guns available. His limited production of a few guns a year is snapped up instantly. Buying a used return-to-battery, or bag gun for the Heavy Bench class is a good way to get into the event. If you're interested in shooting this class a used rail gun can be purchased for roughly half the cost (or less) of a new rifle. Just because it's not new doesn't mean the rifle's not accurate. I used to bird dog for Bob White. When I saw a rifle or tool at a good price at one of the matches I would run over, get Bob, and set him on the seller (set upon is an appropriate term, Bob is a tenacious bargainer). At the Super Shoot in 1983 someone was selling a return-to-battery .308 with a two piece Ferguson rest. Bob bought the rifle for a good price. Fred Finlay picked it up from Bob and let me use it in the 200/300 Nationals that year at Mainville. At 200 yards the largest ten shot group the rifle shot was a .899″. There wasn't a single group at 200 yards with a bullet out of it; each group was round and pretty. That rifle pounded shot after shot into a cluster at the longer distance. Not shabby performance for a used rifle wouldn't you say? Jim Novak had the same experience, Frank Obrochta put a for sale sign on his big gun one year, Jim looked it over, and if I remember correctly bought the entire rig for less than $400. It was another rifle that shot group after group into one hole. Benchrest doesn't have to be expensive, I've proven long ago that ugly equipment can shoot just as well as the pretty stuff, look around a little bit and buy smart.

In the 1988 Super Shoot, to win a 100 yard match trophy in Unlimited it took fancy ten shot groups like the .175″ target by Bill Brawand, the .160″ group by Russ Boop and the .183″ effort by Jeff Summers (any of these groups would be a welcome addition in a five shot Varmint match, but to get them in a ten shot match is amazing). Jeff won the 100 yard aggregate by averaging .2876″ for his five groups. At 200 yards it was just as incredible. Russ Boop was hot the whole weekend and won another match with his .553″, Jerry Masker stunned the crowd with a .390″ ten shotter (with that Jerry didn't win the small group trophy, and check; Mimi Cauvin from France slapped a .386″ downrange). Brad Rosenthal produced a superb .461″, and Paul Johnson snuck in with a tremendous .402″ group. Perry Morton won the 200 yard aggregate with a .3872. This translates into five, 200 yard, ten shot groups averaging .774″. To show you the level of any one of these lofty groups; I've been shooting Heavy Bench in competition since my first year and my smallest ten shot groups are .194″ at 100 yards and .530″ at 200 yards.

The Heavy Bench class helps any shooter interested in the lighter classes. Having to keep ten shots in a cluster is more difficult than keeping five tight. A shooter will become a better wind flag reader, and a better wind doper by striving for close groups with a big gun. Since you won't usually get ten shot groups off in all the same conditions it forces you to use the sighter and hold for shots. Holding into a pickup becomes second nature in the ten shot groups. With it's non existent recoil there's no reason anyone can't enjoy themselves in the Heavy Bench class. Even better practice for the light classes is to shoot a Heavy or Light Varmint rifle in the Heavy Bench class. The ten shot groups really get you in touch with the rifle, its load, wind effect, and quality of your segregated brass.

Ever since Chas. W. Rowland shot his .725" ten shot blackpowder group with a .32/40 in 1901 the benchrest world has been trying to better it. It looks like the day is here when in good conditions we can consistently beat that effort. I wonder what C.W. Rowland could have done with modern benchrest equipment, and techniques.

*Seely Masker has shot cruiser rifles in Heavy Bench for years. With them he's won at the national level, and set a record.*

# 16

# HUNTER RIFLE CLASS

Two different styles of shooting make up competitive benchrest. The first type is group shooting: the shots aren't required to impact at a specific point, hitting anywhere in the legal area a group would get the same measurement. The second type of benchrest competition is Hunter Class, where shooting is for score. Hunter Class targets have a circular target with an X dot, then ten, nine, eight, seven, and six point rings. Hunter rifles are fired to hit the ten ring in the center of the target, with the X dot used as a tie breaker.

Rules for the class are designed to ensure the rifles have something in common with the rifles which we take into the game fields each year. Maximum allowable weight is ten pounds and the cartridge must have at least the powder capacity of the .30-30. Bullets of 6mm or larger are allowed, but obviously, the larger the hole a bullet punches the more points an identical shot will catch. Working safeties (no longer required in NBRSA Hunter Class) and magazines which hold at least two rounds are required. Maximum scope magnification is only six power. You might ask why these limitations like six power, magazines, and working safeties. The class was originally designed so the average shooter, with the average hunting rifle, would have a benchrest class in which to participate. By getting their feet wet in a class which was easy to get into, there was a chance they would become interested, work on their equipment, loading technique, and shooting skills in the hunter class, then move on and become involved in the group shooting classes. There have been quite a few group shooters who followed this route. Some have stayed primarily in hunter class, some shoot only in the Varmint classes, but all keep their interest in score shooting.

*Hunter events are the easiest to put on. Not needing moving backers; small clubs can easily run a match.*

Pure Hunter Class rifles, built specifically for target shooting, can still be used as game hunting rifles. For years the woodchucks in New Jersey got chased by my 6HLS. With a 68 grain benchrest bullet spun in their direction there were a few who wished they had slept late in the morning. Similarly, Ralph Council of Houston, Texas has shot his deer every year with a short .30 caliber he calls the .300 Council. When a rifle's capable of .250″ to .500″ groups every time it's shot from the bench it's easy to drop a whitetail at 150 yards with a neck shot.

Case designs of all sorts are used in the hunter class rifle. The big boomer which probably gets more rifles built for it than the others is the .308 Winchester. By using a tight necked reamer, with the body set for the minimum dimensions of commercial brass, the .308 has punched lots of 250 scores over the years. The most accurate load for the full sized .308 is in the range of 39.5 to 41 grains of H4895. Loaded with the Sierra 168 grain Match King and spun down a 14″ twist stainless steel, match grade, barrel .308s will put their shots into the ten ring any time the shooter reads the conditions correctly. If there's any drawback to shooting the full length .308 in hunter rifle competition it would be the recoil developed. Shooting the .308 usually means holding on to the rifle during recoil. There have been a few who shoot full .308s free recoil. It definitely loosens the fillings over the course of a match when you try that one. Marcy Lyons of Louisiana, who does shoot a .308 free-recoil, commented that it makes up for the pain when you look through the spotting scope and see a pin wheeled 10x staring back at you. Holding firmly onto the .308, having good form and the ability to take the generated recoil, hunter shooters can get a ten every time.

Cases which generated less recoil, with better accuracy, have been in development since the mid 1970's. The first two minimum capacity cases developed for 6mm bullets were the 6X250 Savage, and the 6HLS. With its body taper causing excessive bolt thrust with heavy loads the 6X250 fell out of favor. The various versions of the 6HLS have stuck around and are still in use by many hunter class shooters. The style of 6HLS used most commonly is to cut the chamber with a 6mm Remington reamer held short in the order of .300″ -.320″. Brass is formed from .22-250 or .250 Savage base cases. Test a few lots and use the base brass which measures more consistently in the case head and the neck. The cases for my 6HLS are made out of Winchester .22-250 brass. Using hand held neck sizing and bullet seating dies the cases have over a hundred shots on each case without losing a case to a split, or separated, neck. Velocity with a 68 grain bullet is in the 3250 fps range with H4895, and up to 3500 fps with 760. The best scores with my rifle have all been shot with high velocity loads using 760.

Roger Gower, the premier IBS Hunter Champion, and a host of others have been using the 6X44. The 6X44, another minimum capacity 6mm, is made by running the 6BR reamer in long. A good example of the benchrest theory of getting the best accuracy from a short, fat, case. Brass is formed from small primer URBR brass (.308 brass with a small rifle primer and annealed further down the neck) or from the Federal Match .308 brass with its large rifle primer.

Most of the recent development in minimum capacity cases has been in the form of short .308s. There are quite a number of reamers in the hands of gunsmiths which shorten the .308 case so it develops less recoil for the recoil averse, yet it still punches that .308 sized hole to catch all the points and X's possible. I set up my Remington 700 6HLS with a switch barrel for one of these short 30s. Ralph Council has a version he calls the .300 Council. Using his hand swaged, 109 grain, 30 caliber bullets the cartridge develops much less recoil in comparison to the full bore .308. Enough less recoil that I can shoot it free recoil. Of course it still thumps you a lick, but it's bearable.

## Match Strategy

In group shooting we found the condition to run a shot string in by experimenting on the warm-up target. Testing the prevailing condition, testing the reverse, testing slack periods we would find that the non normal reverse condition would often be lighter and yield better groups. In hunter competition it's still a good idea to test the conditions, but, since it takes longer to resight the rifle between record shots, and between sighter shots (record shots are fired at two columns of bulls eyes, with the sighter bull in the lower right corner), this resighting to different points on the target uses quite a bit more time than would be used in shooting for a group. Usually it means there isn't enough time to run a string of shots during a light reverse condition. You'll find the target is easier to finish if you set up to fire record shots during the prevailing condition.

You'll shoot more tens by treating each bull as a separate match. When your condition comes back go ahead and fire a sighter before the record shot is fired. Concentrate on trying for an "X" on each bull; if the shot misses by a little bit it's still a ten, if you were only working for a ten, and missed by a little bit, it could become a nine.

The type of shooting, either for group or score, a competitor gets into depends on the preferences of the local clubs, and those within reasonable driving distance. If the club just down the road hosts both types of matches it's easy to try both with your own or borrowed equipment and decide which you like best.

Shooters in the Northeast have the best of both worlds. In the Pennsylvania, New York, New Jersey area there are many benchrest ranges within a couple hours drive. It's when you're off the beaten track where the local range preference becomes more important. If you live near Porcupine, South Dakota, you're lucky, there's a range close, but if you're in Moscow, Idaho you've got a major haul to get in any competitive shooting. I got my start in the Northeast. From my central New Jersey home there were enough close ranges to shoot benchrest matches 19 weekends in a row one summer, and a total of 38 for the year (it should be obvious this was before I got married!). The only ranges which were further than a four hour drive were Painted Post at five hours, Kelbly's at eight hours, and Stittsville, Ontario at eight hours. With two drivers that's as far as I'll travel for a two day match where I can't take travel time off from work. Varmint class shooters like Dennis Wagner, Rex Reneau, and Lowell Frei really want to be the best competitive shooters they can be. They'll set up vacation time for travel to the big matches, and spend the rest of the weekends shooting and preparing for the big events. That's one of the reasons the three of them have so much success in the major matches: they've focused on them for a long time, they're not running off to a different match every weekend and spreading themselves thin.

When long distances are involved, and the shooter can't travel to the matches several states away, find out which event the closest range runs and build equipment for it. Another choice is to start your own benchrest league and run hunter matches. It's easy to attach a benchrest section to most rifle clubs and run a couple informal matches each year. Hunter class is the way to go when you're first starting to run matches. They're usually one day events, the average match might only take four or five hours, there's no need for the complexity, and expense, of moving and stationary backers, and the

*The range master runs the show. With a clock, a loudspeaker, and a spotting scope Howard Dietz oversees a smoothly running match.*

changing of targets is simple. Since there's only a single shot per bulls eye one person can run the entire small scale match. Especially when you first start out, try to interest other club members to participate in "shoot what you brung" matches. Who knows, they might enjoy it enough to build first class equipment, and you're on you way to having other shooters to travel with to the long distance matches.

Hunter class involves all the same processes as the Varmint classes. You have to buy or build a gun. When the rifle is prepared it's time to tune the load to the individual barrel. Matching of the brass, bullet, and powder in combination with learning to shoot with good bench technique, and holding shots into the wind, helps you become a better shot. Whether you're interested primarily in the varmint or big game fields, or in moving up to the competitive ranks you'll appreciate the experience.

With the rules requiring a safety and a magazine the most popular action is the Remington 700. Any of the benchrest gunsmiths can rework the 700 and true it up for accuracy work. They will check the threaded areas, and true up the screws so they are perpendicular. Just like in any of the other classes the lugs are lapped for full contact. The face of the bolt will be cut square to the bore, the barrel threads will be square, and tight necked reamers made specifically for accuracy work are used to cut the chamber.

Hunter class's popularity depends on the area of the country. In Louisiana, St. Louis, and Alaska the hunter class is very popular, some of the original hot-beds like Englishtown, New Jersey have slacked off. It's my belief the hunter class can be revived with a change in targets. In .22 rimfire competition they had the same problem as we have in hunter class today. Too many perfect scores were being fired. To make it challenging again the rimfire boys changed from the A17 to the much tougher A36 target. In hunter class, anytime we go to the line and drop a point on the first target it's usually time to pack it in. With average scores as high as they are there's no chance to come back from a fluke gust or reverse which dropped a shot out of the ten ring.

Ron Hoehn has vocalized a similar solution to what many of us have been thinking. On the current 100 yard target a shot can miss by as much as 3/8″ in any direction and still be a ten. That's a 3/4″ group that is still considered "perfect". I don't believe this is right. The target is completely out of proportion to the ability of the rifle, why don't we change the target, make it more challenging, and bring back some of the fun in hunter class. In this vein, starting in 1989, NBRSA will sanction the BR-50 target for score shooting at 100 yards, and rimfire group shooting. On the BR-50 they score "worst edge" of the bullet hole. As Ron Hoehn states it's FUN to shoot.

IBS has two other classes which have proven popular. The first allows the use of the 6PPC cartridge. The second is when we get to use our Light and Heavy Varmint rifles with their high powered scopes on the hunter target. For the shooters who don't have a hunter rifle the varmint class adds a few weekends of shooting: Mainville, or York might have a match on an otherwise off weekend. A popular class for many who like to shoot nice scores, it's run into the same problem the classic hunter class has run into. The rifle capability is way out of whack with the difficulty of the target. I've only competed in the varmint for score class on six occasions. Each time I fired a "perfect" 250. There's something wrong when every time out a "perfect" score is achieved. I've stopped shooting the class since it has no meaning. With an option of shooting a varmint for score match, or to go practice, I would rather shoot groups; something which has some challenge.

# 17

# Case Preparation

Detailed instructions on the segregation, and preparation of cases for use in a benchrest, or accurate varmint rifle. These instructions are for setting up competition quality 6PPC cases using a hand held neck turner. If the cases are being used for a hunting or varmint rifle the turning data is the important portion. Case selection is not as critical a component for factory hunting rifles. This selection information can be used for any caliber, or rifle, for which you want the best cases available. Using the new 6PPC formed to size cases no neck expansion is required before turning. If you're a machinist the neck turning is easily accomplished on a lathe set up with a case holder and a mandrel.

Remember - Safety First<br>
If you don't understand any of these instructions<br>
seek competent help.

## Segregation.

Many top level shooters like Louis Langlinais of Lafayette, Louisiana do nothing in the way of segregation or selection, they just reach into their bag of brass and pull out a handful. The way to win aggregates is through lots of small groups - with a really tiny one to pull the aggregate down. Since it makes me more confident, I get real picky when it comes to case selection. For yourself find the happy median where you feel best about your rifle and components.

To end up with enough perfectly matched cases for one rifle start with 100 pieces of raw brass and plan a rejection rate of four rejects for one acceptance; the rejects aren't thrown away, they're saved till they match with others. In any lot of brass cases there is a bell shaped distribution of

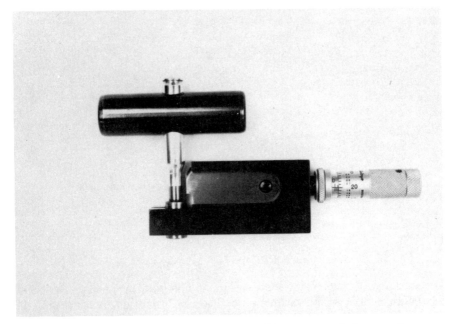

*This Hart neck turner has a micrometer adjustment to help speed set-up.*

weights and thicknesses. Since accurate grouping requires consistent pressure and velocity from shot to shot, I measure and weigh the cases to remove the radical extremes from the record batch of cases. There will only be one or two cases out of that 100 that are so far out they get thrown away. Tests have proven case head runout to be an important factor in the accuracy potential of any lot of cases. We are looking for raw cases with runout of .002″ or less on the case head, this measurement often gives an indication of the distribution of the brass in the case.

Set up a reloading scale directly in front of you on the table. Behind that should be a chunk of paper about two feet wide. When a case is weighed, place it on the paper behind the appropriate weight notation. There will soon emerge a pattern: a few cases will be very light, a few cases will be very heavy. Pick out the cluster of cases in the middle that are all the same weight. Pack the other segregated cases in plastic bags with their weights noted inside the various bags. Next time you weigh cases part of the work is done.

Next step is verification of wall thickness with a tubing ball micrometer, for the most accurate data check this neck thickness around the whole neck. Measure at least four or five places to within .0001″ before neck expansion. An example of the notation might be .0106″ - .0115″. This gives the measurement at the thinnest point, and the thickest point, for this piece of brass. Ball micrometers have a round anvil, this allows an exact measure-

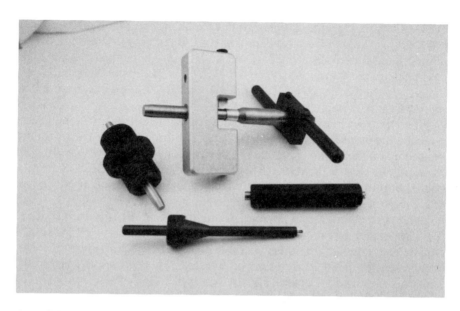

*A tool kit with a Sinclair neck turner, primer pocket uniformer, flash hole deburrer, and neck expander would be a good start for a beginning benchrest shooter.*

ment to be taken. If we tried to use a standard caliper or micrometer the flat area of the jaws wouldn't lie flat inside the curved neck of the case. On a clean sheet of paper run the measurements and set up more brass clusters with the range of the neck dimensions noted. Again, the purpose is to remove those cases that are wildly different from the main sample. (Call these unpleasant souls perfectly segregated cases, and sell them to the hot shooter in your area!) Set up the cases in groups as they are measured. Remember, for an accurate reading the cases must have straight necks, without a burr. Try to avoid it, but if necessary, before expansion use the appropriate full length die if the ball micrometer doesn't get consistent readings.

When this step is finished there will be a central group of cases that's ready for neck expansion and neck turning.

### Expansion

Gather the segregated cases and an MTM plastic box. Mark the box with the specific rifle, and neck dimension of the rifle for which these cases will be used. These cases are for this rifle only from now on. Some rifles, by a good gunsmith using the same reamer, will interchange cases. It's a little more work to set up cases for two rifles but there's peace of mind from having matched cases for a competition shooting iron.

Set up a neck expanding tool in your reloading press. These mandrels and holders are available from Sinclair and Hart. Put plenty of lubricant on the mandrel and the inside of the case neck. Slowly and carefully expand the case neck on the 6mm mandrel. On the multi caliber expanding mandrels, unless you want a .30 x 6 x .22, don't go too far and run the case mouth into the next calibers portion.

When a case is made at the factory the primer pocket and primer hole are punched mechanically from the base side. This process leaves a small burr pushed up on the inside of the case, it's never consistent, usually ending up more on one side or the other. Al Angerman's tests on the effect of primer pocket burrs showed non-uniform flames when the primer is fired. If you don't remove the burr there could be some variation from case to case on how the primer ignites the powder. Removing the burr could be the single most important part of getting cases to shoot consistently. The PPC uses a case with a smaller than normal flash hole. Get a deburring tool made specifically for the PPC sized flash hole and remove this burr. Insert the tool from the mouth of the case. On deburrers which don't have an adjustable mechanical stop only go three light turns after the cutter removes the burr and seats to the bottom of the flash hole. Don't over chamfer the hole. Tests have shown one reason for the 6PPC's excellent results is its small .066″ flash hole.

Use a primer pocket uniformer, as made by Sinclair or Whitetail Engineering, to clean up the primer pocket itself. These tools cut all the primer pockets to the same depth and match the pockets. Primers will get seated to the same extent, ready to meet the firing pin at the same point in its stroke, with the primer cup and anvil square to the impact.

## Neck Turning

We're ready to neck turn the cases, get out a tubing ball micrometer, lubricant, neck turner, and adjusting wrenches. I like to use my old CPS micrometer neck turner. They're now available from MCS in Brookfield, Connecticut. It's easily adjustable, quite accurate, and makes a smooth cut. If you can find one the best (and most expensive) is the JACO made by T.J. Jackson of Austin, Texas. Set up the 6mm mandrel in the neck turner. This is where I like the CPS or a Sinclair, it uses the same mandrel for expansion and turning so the fit is correct. Adjust the cut length. This **must** be longer than the depth of bullet seating in a minimum chamber. This is VERY important. In a tight necked chamber with a minimum clearance case, if the case is too thick where it grips the expansion band of the bullet, there's no clearance and the pressures go through the roof. Don't run the cut too far. Remember you'll change the shoulder location, and shorten the neck, when you fire form it. Compare the new case with the shoulder location of a fireformed case. If you run the cutter too far, and end the cut where the

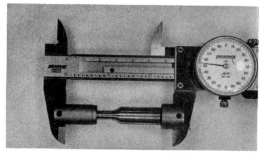

*The Custom Products tool makes primer removal easy. The Custom Products measuring device is popular with many shooters. Wilson case trimmers accurately, and easily, keeps brass the correct length. The Davidson depth checker makes switching bullets easy.*

neck/shoulder juncture will be on the fire formed case; it creates a weak spot where the case will separate in the future. Keep the cut away from the connection by leaving it short, or using a separate, specially ground, cutter to run it up onto the shoulder. It takes a little longer but cases seem to end up cleaner and straighter when the brass is removed from the neck in two cuts. The first cut removes 80% of the total, it also gets the neck dimension and tension just right on the mandrel. That second cut will now be smooth, easy, and consistent.

Lubricate the mandrel, inside of the neck, outside of the neck (lightly). Lock up the case in the handle. Spin the case squarely onto the neck turner being careful not to angle the case and get an inconsistent cut. Measure the case and ensure it's not cut too thin. Brush the brass chips off the cutter blade with a small paint brush. Get some solder brushes from a factory supply store, at a few pennies each they can be tossed in the can after service or stored for next time. Use the same feed pressure and finish up the first cut on all the cases.

Carefully set up the second cut. Adjust and test for the correct cutting depth. A small amount of lubricant on the fingers is enough for the mandrel. Depending on your neck turner it often takes 3 or 4 minute adjustments to sneak up and hit the measurement exactly. Don't ruin a good case by adjusting too far. The adjusting cut is a good place for the cases which were rejected during the culling process. Using them instead of a match case might save a valuable, difficult to replace case. Looking under a microscope shows the blade on some neck turners leaves very tiny ridges when it cuts the brass. When these lilliputian ridges are fresh off the assembly line they can give a false reading by a few ten thousandths on the tubing ball micrometer. The ridges flatten out with the abrasion of a neck sizer button, and under the pressure of the shot. This isn't a problem if you're using sizing buttons, you can change to a slightly tighter button after the first few shots. It causes problems if the cases were set up for minimum clearance tight necks. After five or six shots the cases won't hold the bullet firmly any more. On the cutter I use I set it to cut .0005 thicker brass than the final dimension required.

Finish the remaining cases. Measure after the second and after several to make sure everything is still correct in the measurement department. Clean the lubricant from the inside of the necks with a patch over a rod. Neck size the cases tight enough to hold a bullet firmly. Prime the case with the appropriate primer. Move over to the powder measure: for 6PPC cases made from .220 Russian brass I fill the case to the base of the neck with a fast burning powder like H322. If you're using brass which is not being blown out reduce the normal charge four or five grains for the first fireforming shot. Seat the bullet long, with heavy neck tension so its hard into the lands, and the base of the case is pushed back into contact with the bolt. This helps the case fireform straight and centered on the first shot, in wildcat cases it drastically reduces the chance of headspace separation. The case won't be slammed forward by the firing pin, then have the walls in front of the extractor groove stretched as the neck and forward portion expanded to grip the chamber walls with the base of the case stretching back into contact with the bolt. It's a funny thing about fireforming new cases. In benchrest rifles there have been some amazing groups shot while fireforming new cases. Some people spend the rest of the life of the rifle trying to repeat the fireforming groups. After shooting the cases several times, trim to your favorite length of anything between 1.485" and 1.500", lightly chamfer the case neck inside and out with a Wilson chamfer tool, and pack up for the next match. During the life of the cases check the length every few matches. If the cases have more than a few thousandths difference between them trim back to 1.485" or your measurement and rechamfer.

The competition case is set up specifically and exactly for the bullet to be used, and the chamber in which it's to be fired. Different benchrest bullets have widely different final dimensions with differences of more than .0015" possible between brands. The thickness of the case neck is adjusted accordingly depending on the measured dimension. Custom bullet makers help us out by putting the dimension on the box, but it's still best to check with an accurate micrometer.

The first of two main options for the neck dimension of the loaded round is for it to be several thousandths under the chamber neck dimensions.

*Custom Products adjustable dies make changing the bullet seating depth a snap.*

When the round is fired the brass expands those several thousandths and releases the bullet. For benchrest level reloading a precise, hand held, neck sizing die is used to reduce the neck enough to snugly hold the bullet. Most shooters use a die to reduce the neck .001″ to .004″ from the fired brass dimension depending on the neck tension they want. High quality, hand held, benchrest neck sizing dies use interchangeable bushings, graduated by .001″, so any finished dimension is available. The press dies are out of favor with benchrest shooters. Even though they say benchrest on the label, they're in a fixed neck dimension. If by chance the rifle had the same dimensional requirements as the press die they would be usable. If you already have one on your reloading shelf measure a fired cases outside dimension, and then resize and see what the case is resized down to. If it's resized .004″ or less the die is usable for that rifle.

The second option is tight, or fitted, necks. The loaded round is carefully fitted to be .001″ or .0015″ under the dimension of the chamber. When the round is fired the brass can only expand the .001″ or .0015″ before it meets the chamber walls. This is enough to release the bullet. The elasticity limit of the brass neck hasn't been exceeded, it snaps back to the original dimension after the bullet has exited. Reloading is now a little easier since the case doesn't have to be neck sized. I won't be any more specific on how to set up tight necks. Done wrong it can be dangerous. If you want to set up for them, get an experienced benchrest shooter to go over the fine points.

The third option rarely sees the light of day. George Kelbly and Stan Buchtel sometimes use something called "Stepped Necks". A stepped neck is for those who don't want to neck size or go to the trouble of fitted necks. A "Step" is created by turning a thinner area in the end of the neck. The rest of the neck is left full diameter to create the step. The throat and neck are carefully measured, the brass is turned just the exact amount to get the seating depth exact. The problem with this style of necks comes about if you want to move the bullet out, into the lands, as the throat erodes through use. Then, the cases must be neck sized to hold the bullet further into the throat.

The important thing on setting up cases is to use your head. Set up the cases for the bullet you intend to fire in it. Don't exchange bullets without checking dimensions. I use Lester Bruno's Boat tail bullets. Boat tails don't have an expansion band at their base because of the way they're formed. I set up this .2430″ bullet for tight necks, with minimum chamber clearance. I would run into big pressure problems if I try to switch over to Billy Brawand's .2437″ or .2444″ bullets. Bob White likes to call those .2444s "Fattys". As many have shown "Fattys", being .0014″ over groove dimension, go against conventional wisdom by shooting extremely well, they just need the case neck thickness adjusted to take their measurements. As a final check before firing any new round check two dimensions, use a quality 1″ micrometer to accurately measure the neck with a bullet seated to the depth which will be used. Be positive the loaded round is a minimum of at least .001″ below the neck dimension for that rifle. As a final double check put a dial caliper on the case length, measure the over all length and make sure the neck doesn't go into the leade.

# 18

# Loading Technique and Load Selection

This is the chapter which turns our uncut diamonds into sparkling world beaters that dazzle the competition. For the same reason the 6PPC shoots well, because its a balanced case that brings out the best in the components, the way we run our loading program, and then test for the best load, places the final building blocks for guilt edge accuracy.

The cornerstone of any successful accuracy trial is record keeping; set up a three ring notebook with a chapter for each rifle and a page for each barrel you'll use. Using a full sized three ring binder allows inclusion of match results and sample targets, an option not readily available in a spiral bound book. Organize separate sections in each chapter, with room for notes and sample targets, for the various bullet and powder combinations. Because of their effect on maximum loads notes for weather conditions should include temperature and relative humidity. The perfect load for a cool, damp, morning may develop too much pressure in the heat of the afternoon. As always, safety is paramount, use your head while you're reloading.

Develop good loading habits. Keep the loading area clean and organized, don't change any component without reducing the load and testing for pressure. When you're experimenting with load combinations don't just repeat old habits, keep an open mind for new possibilities, don't reject something out of hand just because the buzz on the street is it's "old hat". Look at Dennis Wagner and Red Cornelison, and their match wins with "old" BLC 1. An accurate load can be among a range of many correct choices. There are a lot more variables in play than we sometimes give credit for; creating accurate results, or poor achievement. The effect of case shape has already been explored. Add to it: the style of bullet, its bearing

*Here's a tool box and loading area set up at the range. Everything's organized for accurate reloading.*

surface, the ogive, the pressure/duration curve of the powder when the primer goes off, engraving resistance of the bullet, and how seating depth changes effect the relationships. Always be aware of the complexity, but don't let that keep you from trying your best to work up an accurate load.

For the example let's start with 15 fresh, fireformed, PPC cases for a new barrel. They've each been properly segregated, neck turned and prepared, shot two times during barrel break-in, trimmed to size and are ready for load development. After cleaning your rifle bring the cases over to the loading bench and spread out the components and tools required. The tools include: a one inch micrometer, six inch vernier or dial caliper, small hammer, neck sizing die with various sized buttons, screw driver, bullet puller, hand held primer seater, powder measure, bullet seating die, primer pocket cleaner, treated cloth to remove burned powder residue from the neck (Hoppe's on a patch, Never Dull etc.) and fine steel wool. The components along with the case are bullets, powder, and primers.

Whenever I fire a group from the bench I replace my empties in the case box neck down, head stamp up. Catching the extractor groove with a fingernail makes them easy to unload into the reloading block. It also keeps any debris (you want a mess, let some kid with an ice cream cone drop his vanilla into your case box) from getting inside my match cases. I pull the cases from the MTM box and stand them in a row, neck down in a yellow plastic 60 hole reloading block. One of my buddies does all his reloading

*This Sinclair arbor press supplies the leverage for reloading with Wilson hand dies.*

from his same green storage box. I don't like using that method. It's hard to pull the cases out of the corners of the box with your fingers, every once in a while a stuck powder charge, or a double charge spills into the bottom of the box. Then you have to unload all the cases and knock out the bits of powder. If they're not all removed a granule could adhere to the loaded round, jam the round off center in the chamber, and cause a thrown shot.

Using a hand-held primer punch, or a neck sizing die with the button omitted, knock out the old primers. After the primers have been removed place the cases on the other side of the loading block. By moving them back and forth it's easy to pick up the operation after an interruption. Most shooters then use a primer pocket tool and a brass bristle brush to clean the primer residue and any powder residue inside the case neck. A swipe with Never Dull, or a piece of treated cloth, removes the external powder buildup. Some use steel wool to remove that build up. It's not recommended: the steel wool slowly wears away brass and can change the neck dimensions over time. There are a few hot shooters who have dispensed with these operations and haven't noticed any difference in group size. Hot shooter Gary Ocock (now that he's moved to Arizona is he even hotter?) says it's been seven years since he's cleaned a primer pocket or case neck. It's funny to watch those who have gone overboard in the neck cleaning department. They'll set up a battery powered screwdriver with a brush and whirr away. Come on guys it's not that difficult. Some people just like gadgets I guess.

The first two operations before shooting a group are to set up the neck tension and initial bullet seating depth. If we're using a competition chamber it will sometimes be smaller than the minimum specs for that round. To repeat, with the advent of loaded PPC factory rounds don't force a factory loaded round and its thick neck where it doesn't belong. Take a bullet from the box, grab your custom bullet seating die, and seat a bullet 1/8″ to 3/16″ into the case. With an accurate 1″ outside micrometer carefully measure the neck where the base of the bullet is (that's where a small ring called the expansion band, the fattest portion of a flat base bullet is). Write down the measurement. Pull the bullet and place it aside for later. We can now figure what size button to put in our neck sizing die. Depending on the neck tension you're looking for, a typical amount to resize is from .001″ to .004″. For our initial bunch of shooting tests we'll neck size the case .001″ smaller than our loaded round figure. This gives enough neck tension to hold the bullet firmly, but not in a death grip. If you can easily spin the bullet in the loaded round increase the sizing amount by .001″ till the bullet resists being readily turned with the fingers.

In a neck sized case with no primer, or powder, use the bullet seating die to set the bullet barely into the case. Measure the over all length (OAL) and write it down. Set up your rifle on a bench top, or in a padded gun vise. Thoroughly clean out any solvent in the chamber and bore. Carefully insert the dummy round into the chamber, bolt the case home slowly. Remove the case and remeasure, verify it's smaller than the first OAL, write down the figure. Remove the bullet with an inertia puller, or the handy Davidson pliers type puller. Replace the bullet barely in the case with the seat die, lock it home again and remeasure. The figure should be the same, do it once more to be sure. To use the phrase I picked up a long time ago from John Ventriglia this is your "Bullet Jam Figure". I'm sure there are other words people use, but it keeps everything straight in my mind. Jacket material is quite soft, and engraves easily. If we used too much neck tension this method wouldn't be accurate, heavy neck tension keeps the bullet from slipping easily back into the case. Conversely, the tension can't be too weak. In that case the lands would grab the bullet, pull it slightly out of the case upon unloading, and give inconsistent measurements.

Set up your bullet seating die to seat to this exact OAL. Pull the top from the hand die (also called the drift assembly) measure, and record the figure. Since it's easier and more consistent, from this point on, we'll be using the length of the top for OAL changes. Set up another case with heavier neck tension, assembled to "bullet jam" length. Polish the bullet in the dummy with fine steel wool. Carefully insert the case and slowly lock it home. Pull the case and look at it under a strong light. Depending on the number of lands, there should be that many faint markings from the lands around the bullet. Use an 8X eyepiece to make this step easier. Adjust the seating stem .002″ LONGER. As the stem gets longer the bullet is pushed into the case, as it gets shorter the bullet is further out of the case. After adjusting the stem polish the bullet with steel wool, lock it down, and inspect for land marks. When we get to the point where land marks just disappear we've found an important point. This is where scads of rifles shoot their best. (Scads should not to be confused with scabrous, the general condition of any rifle I shoot.)

Change the neck sizing button to give the neck dimensions and bullet grip you're looking for. I barely neck size the cases at all, just enough I can seat the bullet in the case with thumb pressure alone. This gives a significant amount of "feel". If a case seats harder than its mates it's moved over to the fouler row, out of the record cases. Lester Bruno neck sizes his cases for a heavy neck tension, but uses the same feel criteria. He notices the amount of pressure required to seat a bullet with his arbor press. Anyone using compressed charges of slow burning powder will need to keep neck tension high enough the powder doesn't change the OAL. To even out this seating drag on the bullet a nylon brush dipped in powdered graphite, then inserted in the neck, does a nice job of evening out the seating pressure. The thing we try to avoid in neck tension is the bullet being so loose it's able to move and change length, or get the point off-centered. My testing shows loose bullets, resting on the powder charge, usually go into the group. The catch word here is usually, once in a while a shot goes searching for Sputnik. There are many individual preferences for case neck tension. This is an area where you should test and settle on something which is repeatable and comfortable.

Use a hand held primer seating tool to seat some Federal 205M benchrest primers. Some like the Remington primers, but the ratio is in the order of 95% for Federal. Don't use the primer seater in a reloading press, they have too much mechanical leverage. (Don't ever use pistol primers in a benchrest rifle. Full bore loads already strain the heavier cup of the small rifle primer. It would easily over stress the thinner cup of the pistol primer.) For best results we want to lightly stress the primer pellet with the anvil during primer seating, inconsistent ignition results if the primer is seated too firmly, cracking or damaging the primer pellet. Using a Lee priming tool, or better quality (and much more expensive) Hart or Sinclair primer seaters, seat the primer by feel to the bottom of the primer pocket. Rotate the case 180 degrees and "kiss" the primer again to make sure it's square to the primer pocket. If you ever seat the primer upside down don't drive it out with a thump from the tap hammer. John Ventriglia got a pat on the back a few paragraphs ago, now we'll give him a kick in the backside. Once John had some empty cases with live primers, and cases with fired primers in the same box. He got a trip to the emergency room when, at a match, he accidently put one with a live primer in his neck sizing die, gave it a whack,

*Frank Wilson gets set to test his reloads.*

and sent the primer cup deep into his hand. Don't let it happen, that primer cup acts just like a little bullet. If I accidently seat a primer upside down the only way I'll remove it is SLOWLY, with leverage. We don't want any impact which could set the primer off. Spray the exposed primer with WD-40, wait an hour, insert the case in a neck sizing die with the button removed, wrap several towels, or a blanket, around the sizing die in case the primer detonates and slowly ease out the primer with an arbor press and base die. Users of the Lee primer tool with the plastic tray should replace the loading chute every year. As the chute wears it allows primers to flip once in a while, with the resultant screw-up when you try to fire a shot. Let me tell you, it does nothing for your concentration, or bolt face, if you drop the pin on a reversed primer.

## Test by Shooting

The hard part of preparing a tack driving load is over, now comes the fun segment: shooting to find the best combination. It should go without saying that doing this next step while the wind is switching and howling is a waste of time. Here's the time to get to the range at daylight, and do your work before the breeze comes up. If you throw rocks at the rooster every morning for waking you before noon it's ok to shoot later in the day, as long as the flags are showing a readable condition. When looking for a match load test various powder charges before adjusting seating depth. Too many competitors fall into the trap of always thinking they need to "work on the load" and end up neglecting the practice during the tough late morning and early afternoon conditions. When the wind is swooping by at all angles and velocities it makes no matter if the smallest group the rifle could produce is .080" or .125". If you've scorned the troublesome practice, and miss a switch worth an additional .250", don't cry for mercy. The target measuring device is as blind as the lady holding the scales of justice.

You'll notice at any benchrest match the shooters all seem to be throwing charges straight from a powder measure. It seems strange at first, but they've all tested and refined their skill with a powder measure till they're capable of throwing charges plus or minus .1 grain in a 28 grain load. My style is to throw three dummy charges into the red plastic top from the MEC bottle which holds the powder in my baffled Lyman/Culver measure. This gets the powder moving through the baffle of the measure. It removes any settling, caused by vibration during the previous parts of the loading process, that would change the thrown charge. Pick up a primed case and place it in the drop tube. The drop tube should be at least four to six inches. Long drop tubes help the powder compact in the case, allowing a larger powder charge in the same volume. I'll ease up the measure lever, gently touch the stop at the top, ease it back down, and carefully cut off any powder kernels stuck in the closure of the powder reservoir. Easing the lever I'll slowly trickle the powder down the tube and into the case. A gentle tap at the bottom of the stroke finishes the cycle. Repeating exactly the same steps I complete the rest of the cases. This style relies on very little vibration and compaction to throw consistent charges. There are a whole range of options all the way to the one Harold Henderson of Houston, Texas uses. Harold raises his powder measure handle to the top of its stroke, whacks it hard three times against the stop, dumps the load and whacks three more times at the bottom of the stroke (and I mean WHACK, you can hear Harold working his measure half the range away). It should be obvious this style throws a much heavier charge for the same measure setting than one with little tapping. Powder measures are adjustable, Harold uses a lower setting with higher powder density to get the same powder charge weight. Tests have proven to him, tapping this way throws even charges in his measure. Test different methods, practice with a scale. Then when you find a style stick with it. Another exercise. Run a little test for yourself. Depending on the pace of the downstroke (dumping the charge down the tube, into the case) or the length of the drop tube, the amount of space taken up in the case can vary as much as the whole neck portion in a PPC case.

Visually inspect all the charges just thrown. Ensure all the cases have powder in them, dump and rethrow any that are at a different level in the neck. By rethrowing these we ensure consistent loading density. What we're trying to achieve is 100% loading density, where the powder barely touches the base of the seated bullet. An added bonus of the 100% loading density is the removal of over or under charged loads. Every so often part of the charge "bridges" and jams in the drop tube or measure. If we weren't close to 100 percent loading density we might end up with load which is too light, by not receiving the whole charge. The next cycle could have dislodged this portion and thrown it along with a full charge into the case. Stuck charges, or double charges, are immediately obvious to the lazy shooters who load right in their cartridge boxes. When a bunch of little black cylinders pour upon an overfilled neck a few minutes of clean up are in order. Bridging isn't a common problem on the short grained powders like H322, or ball powders like 380 and 760, but it happens quite often with the longer sticks of IMR4350 and IMR7828.

If you don't have a high quality benchrest measure, or are still working on the skill to throw consistent charges use a scale for the next phase. There are four main benchrest powder measures. All are repeatable, 50.5 setting on a Lyman/Culver giving X volume today is the same as 50.5 gives X volume tomorrow. When you change powder lots throw a charge on the scale. Different lots often have different densities. Tests have shown the powder which gives the highest velocity with your barrel, case, and components (without causing pressure problems) will usually give the best accuracy. The Lyman/Culver has been my favorite powder measure for many years. The Sinclair, Jones, and if you can find one a Saeco adaption by Seely Masker are all first rate. A measure which has come on strong lately is the Redding with a Sinclair conversion. A few shooters have refined their ability till they get benchrest quality results with the Belding and Mull, but that takes a lot of effort.

For the 6PPC assemble some test loads for three shot groups. Start with 26.4 grains of H322 and increase .3 grain for each three shots. If you're new to the game don't go over 27.6 grains of H322. If any pressure signs appear (loose primer pockets, excessively flattened or cratered primers, sticky bolt) don't even go to this level. The primer and the brass of the cartridge case are a good indicator of the pressure our load is developing, brass flows and distorts under pressure, it's sort of an early warning system telling us to back down. We lose some of the pressure indicators a standard hunting rifle might give. A custom benchrest action has a closely fitted firing pin, without a spring loaded ejector. The shiny ejector mark on the head stamp is one of the first signs of really high pressure in a hunting rifle. A few of the loads used by some shooters develop extreme pressure, they would all have extractor marks if the hole in the bolt face were there. It's a testament to the skill of the action builders, and the materials they use, there haven't been problems.

Get a benchrest gunsmith to inspect the rifle if it's showing any pressure signs from a supposedly light load. Your bad groups while learning will be from missing conditions, or yanking the trigger, not from shooting too light

*Geza Nagy tests everything he can think of. Here he sets out to check another of his ideas.*

a load. The late, great, Nate Boop shot some of his finest scores with a surprisingly light load. If you're setting up a load using T322, with its quicker relative burning rate, decrease your charge from these suggested levels. Clean the barrel after every 12 shots, note which load was fired at which target. I like to use the practice targets Bob White of The Shooters Corner in Hopatcong, New Jersey sells. They're easy to keep track of with six 100 yard benchrest targets on one small sheet of paper, three hole punched they fold over and fit into the loading notebook.

Pick the three best loads and fire another set of three shot groups. Reload ten rounds for the best load from that test and shoot two five-shot groups. If these tests haven't given you a winner start changing the OAL. Adjusting the seating stem .005″ longer moves the bullet .005″ farther off the lands. Inserting accurately measured shim stock under the seating die top is the easiest way to get accurate, and repeatable, moves done quickly. Note - the Wilson bullet seating die many of us use moves the stem .040″ for every 360 degree rotation. I skip the .005 movement and go right to .010″ off the "Bullet Jam" figure. This is where I've found the best groups in my equipment over the years. I've proven to myself I can go into a match cold, set up the bullet .010″ off the "Jam", set the measure to throw 27.8 grains of H322, and be competitive right from the warm-up. If I ever lose a shot with that set up, it's not the rifle or the loads fault; I can always look down range and find which flags changed after I dipped my head to the scope.

If you're just starting out in benchrest shooting and haven't settled on a favorite bullet and powder run the test string for two different powders and two or three different bullets. In my first year I shot several different brands of bullets before finding one which gave me good results and a great deal of confidence. It's good practice early on to shoot as much as possible, every group lays another block in the foundation for later success.

For bullet jump, the outside range beyond which no one likes to be is .040″ off the lands. ("Where no man has gone before", where's Captain Kirk when you need him). In tests .040″ bullet jump will still shoot a few competitive groups, it's the aggregate that suffers. The middle range where a few shooters like to be is .025″ off the lands.

Test the other direction from bullet jam also. Many barrels shoot into one hole with the bullet into the lands. Some pointers. Tests have shown excessive neck tension with the bullet seated long and scrunched into the lands doesn't produce the best groups. A common style is to seat the bullet long, with neck tension loose enough for the bullet to move back in the case as the bolt is closed. This way the bullet is "resting" against the lands, aligned with the bore, and close to the powder in the case behind it. Another common style is to adjust the die to give a particular land marking shape. The common setup for this style is to get a "square" mark from the lands, one which is as wide as it is long. My biggest complaint on putting the bullet into the lands is: if you ever have to remove the round before firing it, the bullet has enough engagement in the throat to pull out of the case and spill lots of little black action blockers all over. If it's safe, point the rifle in the air as you CAREFULLY remove a loaded round from these rigs. If the bullet sticks in the throat gently tap it out with a cleaning rod. REMEMBER TO REMOVE THE CLEANING ROD.

The point to focus on in these load tests is the aggregates for the loads. By keeping careful records compare all the groups shot with each load. We're barking up the wrong tree by choosing a load which in good conditions shot one phenomenal group and three mediocre ones. A load will be better for competition if it consistently shoots worthy groups, but never displays a large one. In the first example the load might not let the bullet "go to sleep". Whenever a bullet exits the barrel it exhibits some yaw. The more yaw, the longer it takes for the bullet to stabilize, the larger the average group. That one tiny cluster could have been a fluke. The other load where all the groups were good shows potential for further refinement and might end up with bug-holes in its future. Keep an open mind, be aware of the information available in the test records. Getting ready for an out of state deer hunt, testing began on my .257 Roberts Improved. It's built on an accurized left-handed Remington 700, Brown fibreglass stock, with a Shilen chrome-moly match barrel. Sample loads were prepared with Sierra 117 grain softnose boat tails and 120 grain Hornady hollow point spire points. The Sierra has a ballistic coefficient of .437. The Hornady's is .388. Hollow

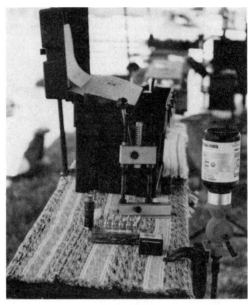

*Another portable loading bench shows organization for the best reloads while at the range.*

point bullets are rarely found on the game fields. This is one hollow point specifically designed to be shot at medium sized game up to 3200 fps. There was a chance for long shots in the Piedmont region of Georgia where we were headed. Going into the tests the presupposed result (call this pig headedness) was to get the most accurate load out of the Sierra boat tail with its .437 ballistic coefficient. Three weekends in a row there were multiple groups shot with the boat tails, and only a few with the Hornadys. The boat tails must have been a bad box. Every weekend the different test loads showed a tendency to throw shots. Every weekend the Hornady groups ended up between 1/2″ and 3/4″. Finally, after all this effort I looked at the notes and targets from the tests. The Sierra would have three or four shots in a cluster with the others revolving, like a moon, some distance away. The spire points were in nice little clumps and clusters. There was the load staring me in the face. I've kept it the same for several years now, made several one shot kills on Whitetails up to 200 pounds, a couple on Pronghorn, and it's still never gone over 3/4″ at the bench in the entire time.

After the most accurate load has been discovered lock down the screw holding the seater stem. There aren't many things more frustrating than finding a loose stem after several groups have been ruined in good conditions. Get in the habit of slapping a dial caliper on one or two rounds before leaving for the firing line. Write down the lot numbers for the components which delivered your most accurate load. Buy a sufficient quantity of each item to last the whole season of shooting. There can be significant variations in accuracy potential between lots.

Powders with burning rates closely matched to the case and bullet combination can be shot into the lands, at the lands, or off the lands, and still get good results. 4198, whose burning rate is a little quick for the 6PPC seems to shoot best off the lands. The theory is that the bullet off the lands keeps peak pressures lower. 4895, which is slow for the 6PPC seems to shoot best with the bullet into the lands. The theory here is the bullet into the lands helps build pressure and get the powder to burn more completely. Don't keep multiple loads in the same cartridge box. The time you slip the mis-matched round into the chamber is always when the range master has just cried "thirty seconds" and the first four shots measured .225" @ 200 yards. Along the same lines set up enough "good" match cases for foulers and sighters. For the utmost in confidence you shouldn't have separate fouler, sighter, and record cases. Take the time to get things right when the cases are matched initially. "If a case won't put a shot into the group what's it doing in the box". Ron Prachyl told me a story from one of his first benchrest matches. He was sitting next an old timer. Several times during the match Ron tossed a piece of brass if that shot didn't go into the group. The guy said: "Son, why are you throwing away that brass." Ron said "It's no good, it threw a shot." He replied : "If you keep that up pretty soon you won't have any brass left." Dave Brennan of East Hartford, Connecticut has a row in his loading block reserved for brass which didn't put the shot where it's expected. He calls them sighters. There are two morals to these stories: first is to look for the condition which caused the shot to take off. Second is, without confidence in the combination we're always looking for the "escape hatch" to shed the blame for a thrown shot.

Benchresters use neck sized cases to get the case fit as perfect as possible. When a round is fired the case expands the slight amount which is available, then contracts back to size after pressures drop. After multiple shots a case work hardens slightly, it has slowly expanded till it gets tight in the chamber, and the bolt becomes harder to close. Tight cases need to be full length resized to reduce the bolt effort. It's desirable to resize the case as little as possible, and to keep the chamber fit as snug as possible. We need to set up the full length die to the dimensions of the case by measuring and adjusting. There are two places on the case which get tight and need to be "bumped". The first is the case shoulder, it needs to be moved back slightly. The second is the portion just forward of the web. The neck is adjusted by the neck sizing die during reloading, that portion of the full length sizing die can be enlarged so it doesn't contact the case. Much of finding out how to adjust a full length die is testing. Donate a sighter case to the task of finding the exact amount to adjust the die. Carefully measure the web and body portion; size the sample case and remeasure the same spots. If the die sizes the body too far get someone with a lathe to lap out the body portion to your specifications. I get my shoulder setting by smoking the shoulder with a candle and carefully screwing in the die till it barely kisses the shoulder and smudges the soot. Then moving the die down a miniscule amount at a time, and trying the case in the rifle, I stop adjusting when the bolt just starts to close easier. Another method for shoulders which doesn't use trial and error is to get a barrel stub cut with the same reamer which cut your chamber. Have your gunsmith put in just the neck, shoulder, and a small amount of the body. Now fired cases can be inserted into the stub, measured, compared to sized cases, and accurate adjusting of the die is possible. Write down the final length of the stub and resized case in your log book for next time.

Full length sized cases using one of these fitted sizing dies have all of the advantages of neck sized cases, without one of the disadvantages. Since the case is only being slightly "massaged" it's still close to chamber dimensions after full length sizing. The advantage of partial full length sizing after every firing is the ease with which the bolt handle works, the speed and tempo available since the rifle stays snug in the bags, or in the case of an unlimited rail gun, the barrel starts to shimmer you can shoot so fast. Don Gentner of Glen Mills, Pennsylvania shot the whole Super Shoot in 1987 using full length sized cases. Testing had shown him there was no difference between his full length sized and neck sized performance.

Being bull headed is the bane of any competitive shooter, (that's similar to being a mules rear end). When the rifle or load needs changing we might toss away several matches while struggling to bend the equipment to rigid ideas. Keeping an open mind and changing things when required keeps the game fun, and interesting. Many who have set up a load in the cool early morning wonder why it scatters shots in an afternoon shoot which might be 30 degrees warmer. In comparison: a load of 760 ball powder for your hunting rifle, set up on an August afternoon might be a little ragged when the deer season gets to 16 degrees.

## Load Trouble Shooting

Trouble shooting becomes easier the longer you stay in the sport. Benchrest shooters, unlike the participants of some other sports, will bend over backwards to help someone in need. There are still times when the rifle has lost it's guilt edge and there's no one to question. Let's go over some of the possible problems with loads and look into a few solutions. The size and shape of the group should give some indication of where to start. Groups with four shots in and one shot out usually mean it's time to try a different brand or lot of bullets, or you missed a condition. Groups with three shots in one hole, then two shots touching a distance away don't indicate a load problem, either the bedding or the scope is moving.

*When you drive to the range the easiest place to reload might be on the back of the truck.*

For a load problem the most obvious questions should be. Has any component been changed recently? Has the fall off been gradual, or all at once? Does it exhibit the fault every group, or only once in a while? Was the thrown shot from a condition and you don't want to believe you missed it? Check brass length, check for split necks, check case neck thickness, check neck thickness for a loaded round and compare it to the chamber dimensions, verify the actual dimensions of the bullet when compared to the last ones (measure them, don't go by the label). Since they often give results which look like a load problem go ahead and check the scope bases and rings for tightness.

The solution to a change in components is apparent. Go back to the items which gave previous good results. A sudden fall off in accuracy means one individual item let go all at once; a gradual decrease could be as simple as a worn out barrel, or bad bedding. There have been many instances where the action glue-in had come loose and it took quite a while for the shooter to discover they were shooting a two piece outfit. I remember this happening two times in one season to Lester Bruno. If the shots out occur once in a while does the thrown shot go in the same area each time? Several times while looking at the batch of targets from a weekend match I've noticed all the groups were measured vertically. Why it wasn't more obvious while the match was in progress is the fault of the crank shooting at the bank. A common trick benchrest shooters use is to recognize that the shape of the group, factored by the days conditions, can give a great deal of information. Groups which cut little horizontal slots indicate the rifle and load are working perfectly, the shooter isn't steering properly. Groups which measure vertically mean the shooter is doping the conditions correctly but the rifle, load, or rests need work. There are several ways to get rid of vertical on a day where it shouldn't be around. The rests we all use shouldn't be a problem if they are of benchrest quality. If the bags are sticking to the stock use a bit of baby powder to smooth out the slide. Double check to make sure there's no contact between the bench and the butt during recoil. The fault could be a bedding problem, then all we can do is turn over the rifle to a gunsmith and let him give it a check. If it's in the load there are two things to try. First is to increase the powder charge a click or two. Don't do this if you're already running maximum loads. Remember to factor in the days conditions before twirling the measure adjusting knob. A head wind might be causing that vertical, you'll spoil a good load, and maybe some cases by going overboard. The second trick for vertical load problems is to test a few rounds loaded with a little more bullet jump. Reset the seating die stem .005" longer, load several samples and shoot them at the sighter portion of the target during the next match. What usually happens is the group on the sighter target ends up about half the size of the collection in the record target.

There are no load development rules cast in stone. Treat each barrel like an individual, find its personality, favorite fodder, and quirks. Forcing it to your pet theories could be the wrong approach, it might be a world beater if treated to the load which matches it best.

Believing more people than not ruin their scores by over experimenting, during a match I've ignored ratcheting the powder measure, or running the bullet seater in and out. Never adjusting seating depth after adjusting to "bullet jam" -.010" the powder charge at no time varies more than one or two clicks on a Culver powder measure (usually down one or two clicks because the day heats up). You can tell when a competitor is adjusting too many things in the components and equipment, and not paying enough attention to the days tricky conditions, when they make a statement something like: "I found my seating depth was off by two and a half thousandths, that's why my last group at 100 yards was .457"; now that I've got that figured out the next group will be in the zeros." Another statement is: "My load wasn't hot enough, the vertical isn't my fault, I'm going up two clicks on the measure." All this while there is a straight head and tail wind which is giving everyone on the range vertical. Joe Vinci, the worst example of this I've seen, will change everything he brought to the match after one bad group. That includes powder measure settings, powder, bullets, scopes, barrels, and probably - his hat, and the oil in his car. Ed Brown of Houston has about worn the click settings off his powder measure. We've been ragging on him about it for years, wouldn't you know, he finally won a few trophies after he kept his hands off the measure (ask Ed about his Top Ten placing in the Gulf Coast 4-Gun). Lots of other shooters change too much, too often, they'll scurry from loading bench to firing line till it's too dark to see. Going overboard on the switching of loads and equipment becomes counter productive after a while. The barrels we use only have a limited accuracy lifetime. It's one thing to be shooting groups in conditions where we are ingraining shooting technique, and another to be spinning bullets down the tube without learning anything.

# 19

# Cleaning Technique

Benchrest shooters have contributed many things to the general sport of rifle shooting. One of them is the requirement for a clean rifle barrel and the techniques used to keep it clean.

A clean rifle barrel has been proven as one of the reasons benchrest rifles shoot 1/8" groups consistently. Many who wander into a group of benchrest shooters wonder why we spend so much time running patches and brushes through those gaudy shooting sticks (when I say gaudy of course you know I can't possibly be speaking of the rifles Fletcher Williams shoots. Rifles painted Clemson Orange with a large tiger paw or the words South Carolina can't be considered gaudy). When a shot is fired primer and powder leave a residue as they burn. This residue builds up after every shot, it can take as few as 15 - 20 shots for an effect on accuracy. For the hunter after an elk or a deer they won't fire 15 shots in a handful of seasons. For a shooter at the bench 15 shots can go by in a matter of minutes. If the residue isn't removed and the rifle is kept in use the side effects are detrimental to accuracy. That powder residue builds in front of the chamber, if it's not cleaned out the residue will be ironed into a compound that's harder than the steel it forms on. This compound can build to .002" or .003" thickness. Once it's there you can't get it out without damaging the barrel. The buildup then sizes each bullet that passes it. Current stainless steel match barrels are manufactured to bore tolerances of .0001" to .0002". Since the sized bullet no longer exactly fits the muzzle portion of the bore, a certain amount accuracy is lost.

There are a few hunting rifles so rough they need their field shots fired from a fouled barrel to keep the first shot on target; however, the modern benchrest rifle will print it's first shot from a clean dry barrel right into the average group. Chronograph testing shows only a few fps loss for this

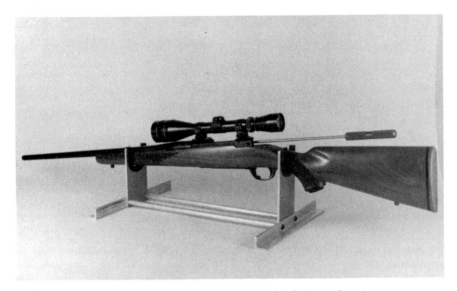

*This Sinclair gun caddy holds the rifle steady during cleaning.*

fouler. During the course of a match I don't fire that first shot into the sighter target until the wind and mirage will give some meaning to the shot, sometimes waiting several minutes. Many people spoil a perfectly good bulls eye by firing that first fouling shot, in a condition they won't shoot anyway, into a clean bull. They might need that mothball uncluttered at the end of the relay as time runs down and they have to make fast decisions. One time at Lafayette, Louisiana there was a man who didn't want that first shot on his target, he would lift the butt of the rifle and shoot it off the backer target. The only problem was, a shot between the target frames clipped the cable that pulled the moving backer - not the best way to make friends! I've seen the cable clipped several times. Fred Finlay and I were trying to get one of Fred's rifles on paper by shooting between the targets at a rock on the earth bank. Well, Fred was unlucky enough to clip that wire by accident.

There are a few items we need to get the rifle clean. First is a rest to hold the rifle steady while the cleaning rod is worked back and forth. It can be a Decker clamping rest, a Sinclair one or two gun aluminum rest, or a homemade rig like Jim Novak and John Jones have made for me. Important things are padding for the paint job and the muzzle below the receiver so solvents drain away from the chamber. Next are good cleaning rods with the appropriate jags. The cleaning rods must be vinyl coated like the Dewey or Parker Hale. A poor second best choice is one of the hardened steel jointed rods. If you use a jointed aluminum rod there's a chance of ruining that

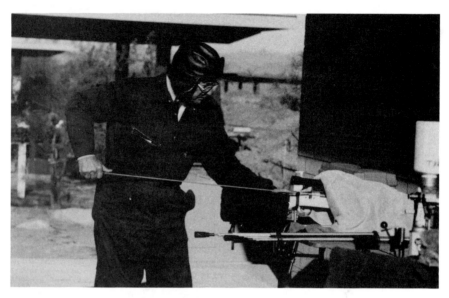

*Alvin Davidson sports the latest in headgear during a surprise cold snap in Phoenix. He also shows correct cleaning rod form with an angled rifle and a straight rod thrust.*

brand new match grade barrel the first time the rod is run down the bore. The soft aluminum can pick up grit, act just like a lap, and scratch the tender lands and grooves with every stroke. If you're not a believer I'll tell you who has done it (it's embarrassing and expensive enough without naming names). You need patches that fit snugly over the jag. Most of us have a favorite type that works well, there's no reason to change.

Solvent is one area where there's been some recent experimentation. The old standby Hoppe's No. 9 fell out of favor when they removed the Nitrobenzene from the mixture. If we look at the danger from Nitrobenzene everyone should cheer their decision. Black powder solvent, Shooters Choice, the new Hoppe's Benchrest, Sweets 7.62, Blue Goop, Quicksilver spray engine cleaner, and JB Compound all have their promoters. Each item has its uses. Black powder solvent on a patch gets out the powder fouling before brushing. Shooters Choice and the new Hoppe's acts on powder and copper fouling. The 7.62 is an aggressive solvent for use on built up copper fouling. Blue Goop is a two part solvent that really works on stubborn copper fouling. I don't leave that one in the bore overnight. Fred Sinclair's tests showed it would pit stainless steel when left in contact for long periods. Someone found the compound in one of the spray engine cleaners did a great job of removing fouling. There's something about the idea that's kept me from trying that one yet. JB Compound is a jewelers abrasive in an oil base that provides judicious mechanical cutting action. The Eubers have used JB Compound as frequently as between every group for their squeaky clean bores. Some of the solvents need oxygen to react with the fouling. Don't use a chamber plug, fill the barrel with solvent, and expect all the copper to disappear. Just like any other item in this sport, read the directions before rushing forth like Don Quixote. If you still need to joust with a windmill I recommend George Kelbly's range during the Super Shoot. There are several hundred windmills to get into trouble with.

The last item, but one of the most important, is a bore guide. Bore guides are fitted tubes that replace the bolt during cleaning. The bore guide fills several jobs at once. The competition two oz. trigger is a sensitive precision device. Any gumming or grit can foul up the works. Just ask Seely Masker how much fun it isn't to have a trigger go bad in the middle of a match. The bore guide extends over the trigger slot and keeps any drips of solvent away from the trigger and the bedding. Make sure the bore guide you use is long enough to get the opening past the action/stock junction. Otherwise, drips can spoil the bedding. The better bore guides have fitted "O" rings that seal the chamber completely. The second important job is to precisely align the rod in the bore. This is why a minimum rod hole custom bore guide as made by Bruno or Jones is a better choice. If the bore guide is sloppy in the chamber, or if one isn't used, the cleaning rod can bow as it's worked and damage the lands just forward of the leade. For a while Rick Hornbeck carried around a cut off chamber where the first inch of lands was missing on one side. Just because you have a bore guide doesn't mean you can put a big bend into the rod and not be damaging the lands. Get the rod straight as it's being stroked. Never - ever - clean a Benchrest rifle without a bore guide!

Let's run through a cleaning sequence so some of this will make sense. If it's been a while since the rifle has been shot wet a brush and rebrush the bore before patching out and shooting. Brushing loosens any gum or dust that's accumulated in storage. After firing ten shots remove the bolt and set the rifle in the cleaning rest. Put the patch jag on the cleaning rod (or for convenience set up two cleaning rods). For a 6mm the Parker Hale .22 jag gives perfect fit on a two inch round patch poked slightly off center, or a 1 3/4″ square patch poked in the middle. Soak the patch with black powder solvent. Push it through the bore once. This one pass removes most of the black grit left from the powder (some people like to leave that grit in the bore for brushing, thinking the extra abrasion is a help). For the rare instance where you think the bore is wet, accidently try to push through a dry patch and stick it tight an inch into the barrel, there's an easy solution. Point the muzzle in the air, dribble some solvent down the barrel onto the patch and jag. Rotate the muzzle and trickle some down each groove to dampen the bore, wait a minute for the solvent to run down the barrel, the patch is now thoroughly soaked and will push through easily.

Change over to the proper size bristle brush. Make sure there are no bare spots and it has a bronze core with brass bristles. I've always gotten good fit, and results, with the Bruno Benchrest Brushes, but there are several suitable kinds. (Never use a stainless brush in a stainless barrel, bore scope inspection has proven just one stroke can damage the barrel.) Soak the brush with solvent and make at least one pass through the bore for each shot that was fired. Never try to reverse direction before the brush passes completely out of the barrel. As you learn the characteristics of the barrel and powder combination the correct number of passes needed to clean the barrel is discovered. Some powders burn very dirty. Between lots of the same powder there can be a big difference in the amount of residue left. I always shoot the cleanest lot of H322 I can find. Dirty burning powder is one reason we use the bronze cored, brass bristled, brush. If the barrel needs extra passes, the brush can't damage the bore. Resoak the brush at least once in the middle of the procedure to ensure there's plenty of solvent acting on the fouling. The easiest method is to use a squeeze bottle with an applicator tip and reapply it with the brush out the end of the barrel.

If it's time to go home; run a dry patch through to remove loosened fouling, resoak with solvent and put the bore away wet. If you're loading at the range; leave the bore to soak as you reload for the next group. When it's time to shoot again start with a tight patch through the bore to remove the solvent and residue. Take a second patch and push it through. This one should only have a light grey smudge on it. If it has heavy black the bore isn't clean, you have to rebrush before shooting. If the patch is only smudged, reverse and push it through the barrel again. This pass will reveal only very light gray. The final touch is swabbing out the chamber to remove any remaining solvent. This is accomplished with a large patch over a brush or a commercial chamber swab sized for the cartridge being used. Rinse the solvent out of the brush, with MEK or a spray cleaner, to make it last longer. Otherwise the solvent will ruin the bristles by attacking the brass just the way it's supposed to. While cleaning, place a paper bag under the end of the muzzle to catch used patches. Clean up any old patches or garbage before leaving; nothing gives a blacker eye to benchrest shooting than leaving a mess at the range.

The bore is now dry enough to put the first shot where it's expected. The best example I've ever seen of a rifle printing its first shot after cleaning in the middle of the group was the 200 yard Light Varmint target Jim Meyer of Torrington, Connecticut shot on September 12, 1982. Jimmy doesn't like to fire fouler or sighter shots. He went to the line and fired just five shots, in a calm, at the beginning of a relay. His five shots at 200 yards measured .155″. An IBS record that stood for three years.

# 20

# *Benchrest Techniques for Hunting Rifles*

Anyone reading this book wants to know how they can make their game shooting rifles group better. If you picked up the book from the rack, looked at the chapter list, and turned back to this chapter - here's one piece of common sense to help your hunting rifle shoot better. Don't let the rifle recoil on the sling studs! I see it all the time, rifles set up with the front stud in contact with the front of the sandbag. You need a bit of room between the stud and the bag, rifles recoil an average of 2/10″ before the bullet is out of the barrel. There, now you've eliminated one reason for poor groups with the old "shootin iron".

We've all been exposed to rifles which cover the whole gamut of potential accuracy. Our shooting pieces may include one or two stock jewels, chambered in something like a .222, 22-250, or 7 Mag, which put their shots into a cluster with nothing sticking out. More likely they're closer to the average, putting most of their shots close, with a flyer or two to spoil the average. Then there's a chance they're rifles more inclined to hit an animal by grasping the barrel and swinging for their head, rather than shooting them. I've never been more frustrated in rifle shooting than when I tried to sight in a Ruger No.1 in 7 Mag, which after three weekends, trying four different bullets and three different powders, wouldn't group better than four inches at 100 yards. That's fine for hitting a moose in the lungs at 15 feet, but it's horrible when preparing for a deer hunt over a winter wheat plot where the whitetails might show up at 250 yards. Needless to say, that tomato stake went back to the dealer in exchange for a .257 Roberts which hit into 1 1/8″ at 100 yards, that's more like it for a factory rifle. Handloads with a Nosler 100 grain flat base pushed by IMR 4064 shrunk the group size

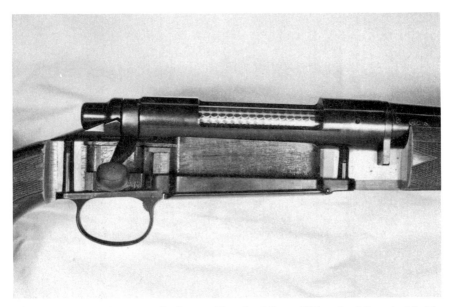

*This cut away shows well done pillar bedding. Pillar bedding is highly recommended for getting your hunting rifle to shoot its best.*

quite a bit from that. The buck who caught that Nosler at 125 yards piled up in a heap right where he had been standing.

Hunting rifles which put all their shots into small clumps don't need a whole lot of work; a factory hunting rifle that gives tight groups is quite a combination, don't screw up the works. Since the rifle you have is probably more like the typical, one that parks a shot in orbit once in a while, let's study the various stages towards getting the best accuracy in the components.

First thing to do with any used factory rifle is to make sure it's clean. Second, put out at least one wind indicator in front of the bench (even a ribbon tied to a tree branch is enough to get started) and try shooting a group with the indicator pushing in the same direction on each shot. If you've never heeded the reverses while shooting groups you'll find an instant 25% reduction in average group size. Most of my practice with bench guns is at a public range. Every time out someone will come up, ask what the streamers are for, then get on a soap box and explain they shoot a .270, or .300 Mag, or whatever with heavy bullets and don't need to pay attention to the wind. Bull.

If you've followed the wind flag advice and still notice flyers out of a central group there are a long list of things to try. Let's check back to the chapter on case preparation and pick out some of the more critical items for use in a hunting rifle. The typical piece used in the game fields isn't

*There's no reason for an accurate rifle to be ugly. This beautiful varmint piece easily knocks the chucks flat.*

accurate enough to need any case segregation other than matching the lot and the brand. Don't go to the public range, pick up discarded brass, and expect it to put all its shots into a dot. Get enough unprimed brass at the same time. Here's a clue. When you're buying brass at the gun store pull out the end flap and check the lot numbers. If the store doesn't have enough, ask if they have an unbroken case in the store room or go to another supplier. There are two things I do to the brass for a hunting rifle which have proven beneficial to accuracy in the typical rifle. The first is internal flash hole deburring. The burr is inconsistent from case to case. Without removing it there's some variation in the ignition curve on every shot. Internal deburrers are cheap, they only need to be used once: when the case is new. I believe deburring is the most important thing in case preparation for a hunting rifle.

The second step is a light clean up of the neck walls with a neck turner. For obvious reasons factory rifles have neck dimensions which are significantly larger than the amount of brass available in the neck of the case. In a factory rifle's large neck there's not as much benefit from neck turning as in the tight neck of a custom chamber. The good which comes out of case neck turning is that the later use of press dies will put the bullet into a concentric neck, and help bullet alignment. If you're using press dies cutting the necks to a thickness so they clean up two thirds of the way around of the neck is enough for factory chambers. They don't need to be cut so thin they clean up all the way around, it would remove enough brass that constant full length resizing would decrease case life. If you've made the plunge for hand held neck sizing and seating dies go ahead and cut the brass for full clean up.

We all know that experimentation with make and brand of bullet might be necessary to find the best combination for the rifle. As it turns out, half the time when we use up a box of bullets which shot like a house afire, and replace it with the same brand, the new box won't perform nearly as well as the first box. The big manufacturers have several machines in a row which are making the same type of bullet. These little projectiles are fed down funnels into a bin which combines the bullets from all the machines. If there are four machines making bullets, and one of them is slightly out of adjustment when compared to the rest, we've produced a box with 25% flyers. Sounds like a good reason for some three and two groups doesn't it? How about when there are two machines out of adjustment? Even the match grade bullets the big companies make are produced on multiple machines. Benchrest shooters have tried to get some match bullets from the individual machines packed separately, but the manufacturer said it's too much trouble. When the rifle isn't to be used for shooting medium to large game, hand made bullets are usually the ticket for an instant accuracy boost. The .22 and 6mm centerfires being used on prairie dogs and woodchucks kill the little critters easily with benchrest bullets at the velocity with which the big varmint cases propel them.

The hand swaged benchrest bullet is available for four of the most popular calibers. In the .22 the bullets are usually in 52 or 53 grain. For $9.00 to $11.00 per box of 100 they're easy insurance against thrown shots that are the fault of the bullet. .222, .22-250, and .220 Swift rifles can shoot these precision made pills quite well without any other changes. For longer range work, or if your sharp twist won't stabilize the 52s, or if you're looking for a little less wind drift try some of the longer 57 to 63 grain bullets from Bruno and Berger.

In the same price range, the .243 is well supplied by all of the custom bullet makers. For those with 12 or 14 inch twist barrels best results might be with bullets from 62 to 72 grains. The hand made 6mm 80 grain pill Walt Berger makes should be the ticket for the .243, .244, and the 6mm wildcats. The latest experimentation in 6mm is for slippery 105 grain bullets with a very low drag. Long range groups could be decreased significantly. Boy, I can't wait till they get released to the public.

Speedy Gonzalez makes match grade 7mm bullets in 120, 140, and 168 grain for $15.50 per hundred. He is also the supplier of great hand made .308 bullets. With weights of 110, 125, and 168 he has all the twist rates covered. Again the price is reasonable at $15.50 per hundred. It's amazing the consistent quality level any of these hand made bullets achieves. For the average hunting rifle in a caliber for which they're made there will be an instant pick up in accuracy potential by shooting match grade bullets.

The next thing to look into after bullets is powders. Most hunting calibers have more case capacity than required. All of the powders in the suitable range can be tried to see which gives best accuracy. Just like in the chapter on loading for a benchrest rifle; start lower than maximum and slowly increase the charge. To quote my friend Butch Wahl of Somerset, Pennsylvania: "Hunting anything which doesn't want to chew on my blue jeans the .257 Roberts Improved does the job". For the same reason so many people go into the woods overgunned, they choose to work a cartridge to it's absolute maximum velocity when handloading. As Butch said, an animal with a hunting bullet through the lungs is dead no matter what you hit him with; or whether it's 200 fps faster, or slower. I've shot several animals with a 180 grain bullet out of a .300 Winchester Mag, and have never recovered a bullet; they zipped through so fast they barely slowed down. What's the use of the extra few hundred feet per second when the bullet will pass through anything we can find south of the Canadian border. Back off that few hundred feet per second and shoot a more accurate load. Plant the first shot in the lungs: trying to put an animal on the dinner table by scaring it with fancy muzzle energy and a sonic crack as the shot whizzes by it's ear only works in John Wayne movies.

If shooting tests after the changes to the cases and bullets have shown promise, but you think the rifle is capable of better accuracy and want to pursue it further there's lots more to do. Several of the items explained in the loading chapter are applicable in hunting rifles. Be warned, use your brain and make sure to approach these tips safely.

The hand held neck sizer and bullet seater are often all that needs to be added to get a factory rifle shooting into .600″ and below. If your factory rifle will shoot the occasional .750″ and the occasional .450″ with the rest in the middle it's starting to show promise. If you've been setting the bullet to the OAL that's listed in the reloading manuals the bullet is sure to be way off the lands. If all your shooting is single shot read over the section about bullet jam and get the bullet closer to the lands: reread everything till you're sure you're doing it correctly. With any hunting rifle, even one that's only shot off the bench, I'll never set the bullet closer than .010″ off the lands. Even then, make sure to decrease the powder a full 10% and work up slowly. If the bullet was way off the lands, and has been moved significantly closer, the maximum load will be reached with a lower powder charge. In a rifle which is only single loaded cartridge length and neck tension can be any figure. In a magazine rifle that's used with a loaded magazine you have to check for two things. First is whether the longer cartridge will fit in the magazine. With a .22- 250 in a long action the box should be plenty long enough. In a .300 Winchester Magnum in the same action a bullet near the lands might be seated too far out to fit the magazine. Second, when using hand dies, is to make sure that the neck tension is set high enough that a round in the magazine doesn't get its bullet pulled out by recoil. Test this by putting one round in the magazine, single load over the top of it, and shoot five shots. Check the length with a caliper, if it's changed the neck tension needs to be increased. This is very important! Don't go into the woods and jam a rifle because a bullet pulled out in the magazine.

One easy way to shrink the average group size from the bench is to boost the scope power. Switching over from a 3X- 9X to a 16X will decrease the groups because you have better resolution, and can be sure you're holding in exactly the same place on every shot. Better resolution isn't nearly as important in a rifle which shoots into two inches at 100 yards. Then, if you miss your hold by 1/4″ on each side of the group you've only increased the group size by 25%. If you miss by 1/4″ on a rifle capable of 1/2″ groups you've changed the accuracy by 100%. Pretty significant eh! Best of all for a big game rifle is to get a fixed power 4X for use in the hunting fields where most of the shots will be offhand and at moving game, then buy a 24X for use at the bench. The 24X scope is a honey for anyone who isn't going to shoot in competition. With a larger field of view, and better clarity, it's more useful on a hunting caliber than a 36X. It's magnification quickly shows if the crosshairs are moving, where before the lower power made you think you were rock steady. If the 24X indicates wiggle city it's time to solve problems in the bench, rests, or hold with their resultant increases in accuracy.

If the rifle still throws shots which are unexplainable it's time to get a competent gunsmith to check things over, and maybe get a bit of work done. Lots of items from the trouble shooting chapter are applicable. Get the trigger adjusted so it breaks cleanly and at a manageable weight. Nothing screws up tiny groups quicker than an eight pound trigger. Get the gunsmith to check if the bolt face is square, lap in the lugs for full contact, check firing pin protrusion, and firing pin spring tension. The chamber must be square to the bore or there's absolutely no chance for accuracy. You could spend lots of money on everything else, but until the chamber is cut straight it's a waste of time. If the chamber is at fault spring for a new barrel. Get the correct twist rate for the bullet you use most of the time. In a .30-06 the factory puts on a 1:10 twist barrel so it can stabilize the 220 grain round nose. If you'll never shoot that bullet put on a 1:12 which works much better with the 150 grain slugs you will be shooting at targets with, the slower twist allows you to try some of the light weight custom bullets which wouldn't be stabilized by a 1:10. My old .300 Winchester Magnum shot its best groups with 130 grain Speer hollow points. Depending on projected use of the rifle get the chamber cut with a reamer made to tighter specs. Killing two birds with one stone always made sense to me.

Since it's not that expensive, and makes a rifle much more stable in the hunting field, spring for the cost of a pillar bedding job. Pillar bedding removes most of the worry during a sloppy wet bear hunt about whether the rifle has shifted point of impact. To really get rid of moisture related impact shifts go full boat and get a synthetic stock for "Old Betsy".

Decide in your mind the exact purpose for a rifle before going out and spending lots of green stuff on it. Is the gun to be used for shooting targets only, shooting game only, or a bit of both? Of the eight rifles I own there are five benchrest rigs which are capable of World Class accuracy. Money and effort to make them as accurate as possible will be spent at any time, in any amount. The other three are hunting rifles in .257 Roberts Improved, .270, and .300 Winchester Magnum. The .257 is capable of the odd group below half an inch. The other two average just over an inch. Brad Harrison of Richmond, Virginia about fell off his chair when he heard I had a rifle in my closet which didn't average under an inch. As I stated to him: "They are still quite accurate, they rarely go over an inch and a half, yet they've never failed to bring down an animal they were pointed at". The five big game animals shot with the .270 have never traveled further than the distance it to took them to skid to a stop on their nose! I know the two big bores will never be shot more than a few shots before the season to check that the impact point hasn't shifted, then during the season they only get fired one shot, twice if I have tags for two animals. See, I know the purpose for the two rifles, they fill the bill perfectly.

Make up your mind what you'll be using your rifle for and what's necessary to fit it into your plans. If it will never be taken into the game field, but will spend lots of time at the bench, decide right off whether it makes sense to put money onto it. Spend the time to calculate whether a Remington 40X, or 700, or Ruger 77 will be that much better after you throw all your dollars at it. Think back to some of the earlier chapters. For target use alone a good used benchrest rifle can be purchased in the $500.00 to $750.00 range. A used benchrest rifle which is almost brand new might only go for $1000.00, if you add up the $300.00 or more you can get out of your used stocker there's not that much to upgrading to a pure target rifle, it makes a lot more sense than spending another chunk of money trying to refine a rifle into something which will only get to the higher lever with a significant infusion of cash. Half the competitors on the line at a benchrest match went the route of converting a 40X to a pure benchrest rifle. They'll all tell you, for pure target work, it's a lot more expensive going that route as compared to getting a custom the first time around. (Or getting someone else to spend the money reworking a 40X and buying used at a reduced price.)

However, if you'll be shooting mostly at critters it wouldn't make sense to get a pure benchrest rifle. For field use their flat bottomed forend, two ounce trigger, and lack of a safety makes their use limited. I've used single shot benchrest rifles to shoot woodchucks and the occasional turkey. It's a hassle not being able to lock home the bolt till the instant before the shot.

Using a Remington 700 as a base you can build a beautiful little hunting rifle which still shoots good groups, yet has a safety and a magazine. With a synthetic stock the weight can get down to as low as you want it. Humping through the mountains is easier with a six and a half pound .308. If the rifle's to be used on small game up to the size of Coyote's get it accurized and barreled in one of the accurate cartridges. The .222, or the .22 BR are good choices. We know the potential of the .222, but the BR is a sleeper. Talking to the single shot handgun boys, they tell of getting 3500 fps out of a 15″ barrel with it. All this and sub 1/2 MOA potential! The bullet from a .22 BR, out of a 24″ barrel, really tears up the woodchucks. It's significantly more accurate than the .22-250, or .220 Swift that's usually used in the fields. In the 22 BR I've had groups below .200″ at 100 yards using a stainless steel barreled, accurized, Remington 700. A well done .308 has the potential of an occasional group that small. Big boomers like the 7 Mag and the .300 Mag won't usually get a sniff at targets quite that tiny, but with the right components and lots of work, groups between .300″ and .400″ are attainable.

Shoulder busters from .300 Winchester Mag and up should all be shot with a sissy bag when used from the bench. Using one of the square, flat, bags from Protektor makes more sense than bruising after a couple shots. Last time I shot my .300 Winchester Mag it was stuffed with Nosler 200 grain Partitions and a bunch of IMR 7828. Two shots at the bench, the day before a hunt, were enough to raise a bruise. The flat bag increases gun weight by a couple of pounds and spreads the recoil over the entire 4″ X 6″ area. It makes shooting one of those big crackers easy. The week before there had been a guy at the public range who was asking for help sighting in his big magnum. He commented: "You shoot it, I'm too bruised from last week". Doesn't sound like fun does it!

Another way to save money is to look over the used hunting rifles on a benchrest gunsmiths resale rack. Serious accuracy buffs are always experimenting and trying to get more accuracy than what they're shooting now. Unless they're rich they finance some of these experiments by trading in good shooting guns. I've seen lots of reworked hunting and target rifles which would satisfy the requirement perfectly, for sale for a lot less than it would cost to build the same thing from scratch.

Give serious consideration to a switch barrel gun. Think about having one action accurized, put it into fibreglass, then have two barrels chambered for it. As an example, make one .22-250, and the other 7 Mag. Even with two bolts the cost won't be that high, and you won't pound yourself silly shooting the magnum at targets every weekend. When it comes time for hunting season switch barrels, and scopes, and head for the hills.

If you're interested in learning more about the latest in rifle accuracy buy the compilation that PRECISION SHOOTING has released. They took the best articles from the last eight years and put them all into one "super magazine", now rather than having to buy 90 magazines at a couple bucks each the good how-to articles will all be at your fingertips for under $10.00. Another thing to get is the catalog from Sinclair International. It supplies a wealth of information. Fred Sinclair carefully explains how to use all the tools, the methods, and the reasons for it. If you're just starting in accuracy reloading Sinclair offers package deals of the popular tools. A couple of evenings reading the magazine and the catalog will make you one of the most knowledgeable shooters in your club. You'll be amazed at the tips those articles divulge.

My friend Dickie Pustejovsky from Huntsville, Texas commented that he has been reloading, trying for good groups, and shooting high power rifles for 15 years. After a brief exposure to benchrest techniques, tools, and equipment he realized the previous 15 years were only grade school compared to where he is now. "For 15 years I only thought I was shooting." What these comments show is that the national magazines don't give a true picture of the accuracy that's available from a good rifle. Hook up with a subscription to PRECISION SHOOTING, then go to a benchrest match and look at some of the things shooters are doing to get their rifles to shoot into one hole. Ask questions, get a few phone numbers, find who shoots at a range close to your home, and start figuring out how to get your rifle to be the best it can possibly be. The match is a good place to put out the word that you're looking for tools, scopes, equipment, and advice on how to get started on the right foot in the accuracy world. There's always a bulletin board at a match where you can post a card with your requests. Have a spot for the shooters to write where you can find them, and get together for a bull session while they're waiting for their relay. Heed the advice that's given, I remember the follies of one bull headed shooter. He had a problem changing some of his preconceived notions about what should go into an accurate rifle. After prodding, poking, and scrutinizing a used benchrest rifle Bob White had on his resale rack, this guy decided to have Bob build him a hunter class .308. But, after seeing heavy finger pressure could slightly deflect the sides of a fibreglass stock he decided the stock was too flexible: "Don't you think this stock is punky". Not listening to Bob and I (and about five other guys) he had the stock built with two layers of fibreglass and extra amounts of resin, so in places the stock was almost completely solid. The special order stock came in, the action was bedded, and checking on the scale showed the rifle would be more than a pound overweight if a normal taper barrel was put on. In order to make the ten pound weight limit for hunter class competition the barrel had to be shortened and reduced in diameter, an obvious detriment to accuracy as compared to any perceived "punkiness". Don't be bull headed about what makes a rifle accurate!

# 21

# *Troubleshooting*

At one time or another a rifleman bumps into a shooting iron with accuracy potential, which refuses to shoot good groups, or one which has shot good groups, but lost its edge. Listing and discussing some of the things to look for might give you a bit of a handle on the various possibilities and save some time, money, and frustration. A hint to the new purchaser of a benchrest rifle who isn't experienced in the use of wind flags, and calling shots. Get an experienced hand to try one or two groups with the piece. Shooting over flags, they will know whether the shots stepping out of the group are condition influenced, or equipment trouble. Unnecessary tear downs use up time which could be better spent punching holes in a target.

The best (or worst) example for needing to get an experienced opinion comes from one of Bob White's customers. This fellow had Bob build him a rifle, being particularly strong minded he had Bob change several of the standard features usually found in a competitive rifle. After a delay caused by the wait for non standard components Bob built up the rifle, shot one round on his home range to check function, and sent the gent merrily on his way. The excited telephone call which followed showed a complete lack of common sense. Seems the guy had taken this rifle to his local underground shooting tube range, and after bore sighting (or so he thought) tried to fire at the 100 yard target. He complained loud and long that Bob had built a rifle which couldn't be sighted in, he said the rifle was so inaccurate shots hit the sides of the tube, rather than the target at the end. He commented: "The club president was there and he couldn't hit the paper either". This sure was a puzzler to Bob, but since he guarantees his work he immediately requested the rifle back for testing. Tests showed the scope was so far out of bore sight, bullets were hitting several feet away from point of aim at 100

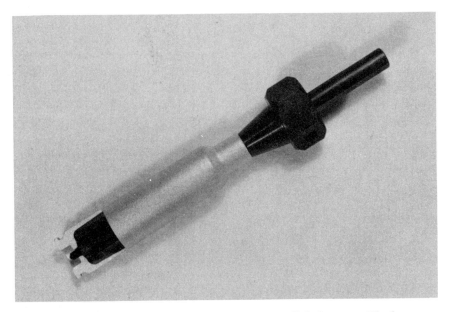

*This internal deburring tool from Sinclair will help any rifle be more accurate.*

yards. After bore sighting and one sighter Bob shot a .350″ five shot group. I would love to have a hunter rifle that inaccurate.

There are two different types of rifles which won't shoot. The first is one with no history that's been purchased, either new or used, and testing gives poor results. For a World Class 6PPC with a custom action, synthetic stock, match grade stainless barrel, and two ounce trigger poor results might mean the rifle shoots groups that average .300″ to .500″ in good conditions. The second type of rifle is the one which you've been shooting for a while, and it either gradually decreased, or stopped grouping all at once. The first thing to do; especially with the newly purchased used rifle is to ensure it's clean. The average shooter doesn't know how to keep a barrel clean, and often times when they do use the proper solvents, rods, guides, and brushes they shoot too many rounds between cleanings. Even if the seller told you the barrel only has 500 rounds through it, they might have only cleaned the rifle ten times! If you've read this far into the book I hope the first thing you did after acquiring the rifle was to soak the bore with solvent and give it a thorough brushing. If the patches show heavy copper or powder fouling, a good clean-up with one of the stronger solvents might be the ticket to get the stick shooting again. If the barrel is clean there's a long list of things to check to try and correct the problem. If you're doing the work at the range, or are lucky enough to have a bench right outside the workshop - correct procedure insists checking, and testing, be done one step at a time. If it's over an hour to the range, as in my case, look for an obvious problem, and try to fix the puzzle all in one shot.

Buying a used bench gun usually means some brass comes along with the rifle. A novice, more often than not, doesn't get the brass neck dimensions or seating depths correct. Check these two things first. It's obvious you've found a big chunk of the problem if the cases have the bullet seated a quarter inch off the lands, or the loaded case necks are oversized for the chamber.

More often than not I've isolated the problem by working with the scope and its mounts. Minute amounts of movement in a scope base translates into significant error at the target. Pull off the scope; remove the rings and bases. Pulling the screws from the bases is very important. Lots of times it's a too long front base screw contacting the barrel which causes the conniptions. Look at the bottom of the screw, and on the barrel, for shiny signs of wear coming from contact. Because of their removal of a critical area for bewilderment I love actions like the Kelbly, and the MCS, which have their bases machined right into the top of the receiver. If the screws weren't contacting anywhere, apply some thread locking compound to the bases screws and tighten them up with a properly fitting screwdriver. With the bases and ring bottoms tight switch to a scope of known performance. I'll go to the range and check for grouping ability at this point. It's often the solution, and it keeps us from doing anything drastic to the rifle.

Get an accurate torque wrench and check the stocks screws on a bolt in. Max for the front and middle screw is 40 inch pounds; max for the back screw is 25 inch pounds. Check that the barrel is tight in the action. Several cases a year come to light where the barrel was so loose it could be twisted by hand. If the barrel had been loose remember to full length resize the cases before trying to shoot again. They've become longer by at least a few thousandths, in essence they've been fireformed into a long PPC. Testing has proven inconsistent contact between any of the rifles individual components is detrimental to accuracy. Look at the obvious things first. Put the rifle in the rests (to set up the same stock loading as found during firing) and run a piece of thick paper down the barrel channel, ideal clearance is .040″ -.050″. Is the barrel really free floating all the way, or at least to within one inch of the action, where the bedding starts? Is there any contact between the bolt handle and the stock, if there is the hand rubbed paint job has to go; relieve the area to remove the contact. Check the trigger housing, make certain it's not hitting the stock anywhere, look at the trigger as it's released, make sure it's not contacting the trigger guard.

On a bolt-in, if it still doesn't shoot pull the action screws and check them for contact at the tip. Probe the action bedding with a pointed tool, look for soft areas caused by dripped solvent. Any areas of rubbery bedding points to the cause of the poor targets. Gummy bedding is common in rifles which are cleaned without bore guides. Even with bore guides tight patches soaked with solvent often lay a drip onto the butt, behind the action. This

*Benchrest shooters like Myles Hollister epitomize benchrest. He's a great guy, a fine gunsmith and bulletmaker, and a tough competitor.*

was the cause of my 6HLS's trouble punching tens one season. When the action was removed from the stock the epoxy bedding had a film of solvent over it, so no matter how tight the stock screws there was some movement between different shots. Clean with a towel over the butt stock, or close by, to catch those drips and keep them out of the bedding.

On a glue-in there are a couple of non destructive ways to check for glue-in failure. Put the barrel into a barrel vise, and gently grip the forend and barrel together with your hand. If the epoxy has separated it will often show at the rear of the action, between the bolt slot, and in the port cut. Don Gentner checks his bedding with a Paul Bunyon act, he grabs the rifle stock and swings a big arc that results in the barrel slamming a wood table. He figures if the bedding holds after that test it's ok. The only way to check the bedding completely on a glue-in is to pop the action out of the stock and give it a once over. If the rifle is a tack driver, don't fix something that's not broken, in this case we're working on a rifle which isn't shooting, so it's ok to mess around a bit. One of my old motorcycle buddies had a bad case of the "fix it before it's broke" syndrome. He would change the oil in the front forks of his Bultaco Alpina three times a day "to make sure it's clean". After two days of this (with the rest of us telling him he was nuts) he stripped out the phillips screw from the drain hole!

Some of the big time gunsmiths recommend reworking the glue-in every one or two years anyway. It shouldn't hurt a rifle which is a "shooter", and it might catch one that's just starting to go bad. The flip side of the story is: beware of removing glue-ins, it's possible to break the stock, or damage the action.

A rifle purchased used likely has some barrel damage. It's usually caused by improper cleaning. Jointed steel rods thrust through the bore without a bore guide can damage the leade, the lands, and the crown all on the same stroke. I've heard of people who ruined match barrels with steel rods on the first cleaning! Pulling the barrel off and eye balling it can give a hazy indication of the "alligator hide" look. If it's there in a 6PPC the rifle's probably had more than the 500 rounds you were told it had, and it might be time for a fresh barrel.

Proper alignment of the witness marks on switch barrel guns is more critical than a one barrel gun, witness marks can't be stamped in till the threads have been stretched to shape. If you have a benchrest gunsmith close by crown damage can be cleaned up easily, and quickly (it's cheap compared to any other operation on the lathe). Recrowning to remove damage can have significant impact on a rifle's grouping ability.

There's a few things with the cases we can look into. You'll need an accurate dial caliper, tubing ball micrometer, and standard 1″ micrometer. Review the chapters on loading and case preparation for the answers to these faults. First thing to check, as we've discussed earlier in the chapter, is the over all length, and the neck clearance. See if the inside of the flash hole has been deburred. Check with the tubing ball micrometer to see if the brass was neck turned consistently and to the correct thickness. I've checked brass others have cut on numerous occasions, one time I found several thousandths variation between the high and low dimension. Several thousandths is worse than some factory brass! (To top it off, the case looked like it had been cut with a dull garden trowel.)

The bolt deserves some attention, I'll hit the high points on what to look for, bolts need to go to the gunsmith for reworking if it's the problem. The firing pin should strike the center of the primer, every once in a while a bolt comes out where it's firing pin hole wasn't drilled in the center of the bolt. This will crop up more often in the production action, but it's happened once in a while in custom actions. (The flip side: Tom Gillman had a firing pin so far off center he had to index the primer so the pin would strike one of the legs of the anvil, and look at everything Tom won!) The bolt face must be perpendicular to the bore, the lugs need to be making at least 75% contact in the receiver. Bolt-barrel interference gives strings all over the place as the barrel heats up. Check the case head diameter, make sure there's at least .005″ clearance between the rim and the edge of the inside of the bolt face.

Let the gunsmith measure for proper firing pin protrusion, and firing spring tension. Finicky types keep track of the firing spring tension by testing it each year. They grab two pieces of wood and a bathroom scale.

Then drill a hole, that's a bit larger than the bolt handle end of the firing pin assembly, halfway into the bottom board. This is the board that rests on the scale. The top board needs a stepped hole, the first hole lets only the firing pin through. The second portion of the hole only goes halfway through the board and provides a stop for the shoulder to push on. Apply pressure with the top board till you feel the spring begin to depress. It's normally in the 17-18 pound area. Slowly apply increased pressure till the spring reaches maximum compression, usually at around 25 pounds. Remember bathroom scales aren't perfectly accurate, so record the figures and compare them on the same scale next year. Weak springs should never be a problem on any of the custom or recently manufactured actions. It's only in the case of something like an ancient 98 Mauser that poor springs are the culprit.

There are a few rifles which shoot as wild as old time Dodge City on a Saturday night. Careful checks of everything previously mentioned shows no flaws, a bore scope indicates a good barrel, the chamber was cut correctly, the action is trued, switching between scopes shows no improvement. It's time to look for a few of the really insidious faults. Take the assembled bolt and carefully rotate the firing pin assembly down the cam, into the fired position. Look for excessive contact between the side of the firing pin head, and the side of the bolt body. Extra contact here creates drag when the pin is released, with its consequence of inconsistent ignition, and erratic performance. If there's contact a gunsmith can adjust the bolt body slightly to supply the proper fit.

In a Remington style bolt the amount of bolt rotation as the bolt handle is closed is controlled by the location of the bolt handle. Over or under rotation can push the firing pin head into contact with the bolt body, align the bolt head to contact a piece of the cam during its firing stroke, or cause a locking lug to bottom out. In the Remington, CPS, and a few others the bolt handle location is set by silver soldering the bolt handle on while in a jig. Some bolts use both screws and solder, some use only a screw. Like any mechanical process there's a chance the jig was slightly out of alignment during soldering, leaving the bolt a snit (for an explanation of what a snit is see Rick Hornbeck) out of position, with the result of the bolt closing too far, or not far enough. Both situations get some more Dodge City shots. The way to check it correctly is with the trigger removed, and measure with all the pieces in their proper position.

One more thing to check, a real bummer till you find it, this one can cause Dodge City, and Abilene, Saturday night shots. The firing pin could be retracting too far into the bolt body, this pulls it out of the firing pin hole, and leaves the firing pin without an exact guide on every shot. One shot the pin might be perfectly centered and strike the primer correctly, the next shot the pin might glance off the edge of the pin hole and result in slightly different ignition characteristics. The pin hitting the edges of the hole causes excess firing pin wear and might bend the pin as well as its ignition problem. Check for it by comparing the distance to the retracted pin in the assembled bolt with the depth of the pin hole after removing the firing pin. If the pin is retracting too far get the bolt to a gunsmith and let him fix it, or send it back to the manufacturer.

With nothing so frustrating as a rifle which should, but doesn't, shoot these comments might help save wear and tear on the competitive spirit by catching problems before they carry too far.

*Troubleshooting can catch problems early; solve them and you can end up in the winners circle.*

# 22

# *Current Accuracy Levels*

Modern Benchrest rifles are the most accurate rifles in existence. There are three statements the uninformed make when you show them a tiny target from your pet shooting piece (something on the order of a .088″ @ 100 yards or a .255″ @ 200 yards). The first comment is: "Yea, I have a .243 (or .22-250, or 7mm, or .416 Rigby or whatever) that shoots groups like that". The second statement is: "Anyone can shoot a group like that with the rifle set up on rests like you guys use". The third is: "But, you missed the bulls eye", as they point to your tiny bug-hole nestled between the ten and nine rings. Talk is cheap, I've never been able to get any of these mouthpieces to show the accuracy they can get from their miracle producers. Taking a benchrest rifle to the range on a calm, overcast, day is one of the most pleasant moments in the shooting sports. The rifle, with a little bit of guidance, will shoot group after group into one hole. A moment even finer is when the conditions are horrible, the wind is howling, the mirage is dancing, and a few competitors on the line still pound in those little groups, even though you know a reverse is worth an inch at 100 yards.

There are many old rifles, still in fine shooting form, to show that some of the benchrest shooters of a few decades ago had rifles that would put all their shots into one hole. I've fired several 25 to 30 year old big guns with wood stocks, and externally adjusting scopes, which grouped every bit as well as I was capable of shooting them. If they were done correctly back then: a stable piece of wood, with a stainless match barrel, using hand made bullets, many of yesteryears shooting irons could step up and be competitive on the line today, the only change being to an internally adjustable scope. That's one of the fun parts of this sport. Records are made to be broken. The long time competitor tries just as hard in this decade to break the new records as they did in the last.

*Allie Euber has proven himself worthy of the title Champion. As the winner of many National Championships, and the setter of multiple World Records, he's another credit to benchrest.*

Read the front dust cover again. It states: the modern Benchrest Rifle is capable of a sub .200″ five-shot 100 yard group every time it's fired. This isn't just a reflection of the front pedestal and rear bag on which repose the rifle. It's not just a fact of the modern bullets, primers, or powder. The performance of modern rifles has a lot to do with the man guiding the bullets into one hole. We've discussed the effects of wind on the bullets flight. Now we'll consider the shooter, on the top of his game, who uses the sighter target, watches the wind flags, who aims at three or four different spots and lets the wind push the bullet into a tiny one hole group. Technical advances have corrected a lot of the historical problems experienced with the average benchrest rifle. At least half, and probably more than half of the rifles we find on the line at any given match are capable of groups approaching record levels. It's the wind, mirage, nerves, and the management of them which gives a shooter match winning, and record setting performances. One of the most pleasing things about records is, they aren't all set by men. In 1953 Olive Walker held the world record for 10 shots at 100 yards, a .3268 group she shot with her .222. For a while Donna Lee Price held the NBRSA Sporter record with a .090″ 5 shot group she shot on September 4, 1972. Lately, it's been Faye Boyer who's put the leather to a few with their nose in the air. Winner of many matches over the years, in 1987 Faye was the NBRSA Heavy Varmint Champion.

*Homer Culver and Red Cornelison show there's no generation gap in benchrest. Both have proven capable competitors in careers that span decades.*

In order to be considered for a record, a group, or aggregate must fulfill several rules. First: it must be shot at a registered match with moving backers. Moving backers are strips of paper, or cardboard, which slide horizontally behind the target while the group is being fired. They reveal the proper number of shots really exist in that tiny bug hole. The targets must be signed by the match referees, verifying they've looked at the target, checked the number of shots in the backer, and certifying correct procedure was followed. Each benchrest organization maintains a Records Committee. The targets are forwarded, with the paper from the moving backer, to the committee for official scoring. The three official scorers each measure the targets. These three measurements are averaged. If the result is below the existing record, it's recognized, and recorded as such. These rules are stringently enforced. Several times in the past potential records have not been recognized because of errors in following the guidelines. It's up to you as a competitor to make sure all the necessary steps are complete before submission for official measure.

This chapter recognizes some of the shooters who spent time working on their equipment, and shooting skills, and have achieved record setting performances, or been inducted into the Benchrest Hall of Fame. Many others not listed here have held one or more of these records over the years. Some scores have been broken several times in the same weekend. Some are broken once or twice in a season. A few have held for decades. There is no greater thrill, and confidence builder, than to say: "I shot a World Record".

## PHOTO CREDITS

# Benchrest Glossary

## A

**ACCURIZED**   Term for the careful reworking of a production action, or rifle, for better grouping ability.

**ACTION**   The heart of a rifle, the combination of the receiver, into which the barrel is threaded, the trigger is attached, and the bolt resides.

**ACTION WRENCH**   A tool inserted into the action, which combines with a barrel vise, to provide leverage for unscrewing a rifle barrel.

**AGGREGATE**   The combination of groups into a final score, considered as a minute of angle (1″@100, 2″@200) ex. 100 yard groups of .155″, .273″, .244″, .341″ and .287″ added together and divided by five would give a 100 yard Range Aggregate of .2600. 200 yard groups are added together and divided by ten, ex. .545″, .672″, .827″, .627″, and .821 give a 200 yard Range Aggregate of .3492. See also Grand Aggregate, and Two Gun Aggregate.

**ANVIL**   The portion of the primer on which the firing pin crushes the primer mixture and causes ignition.

**ARBOR PRESS**   Used on hand dies to supply mechanical leverage for the reloading process.

## B

**BACKERS**   See moving and stationary backers

**BAG GUN**   A heavy bench rifle which is shot off sand bags rather than a return-to-battery rest.

**BARREL TENON**   That portion at the rear of a barrel which is threaded to screw into the receiver.

**BEDDING**   The process of getting a very close fit between the action and the stock. Benchrest rifles are usually glued directly together with epoxy.

BLOW      1. A very heavy wind
2. Rounds loaded over maximum can "blow" a primer, the primer pierces at the firing pin indentation.

BOAT TAIL      A style of bullet with a taper on its back end. With less drag than a flat base it retains velocity better at longer ranges.

BOIL      Vertical mirage, from rising heat waves.

BOLT HOLSTER      A leather or nylon pouch, carried at the belt, for holding the bolt any time the rifleman's not on the firing line.

BOLT SHROUD or BOLT PLUG      The portion at the rear of the bolt which keeps the firing pin in line for trigger engagement. In the event of a case rupture it seals the bolt ways and prevents the escape of gas into the shooters face.

BORE CLEANING      Brushing the inside of the barrel with solvent to remove powder and copper fouling. At no point do benchrest shooters go over 20 rounds without cleaning the barrel. Always patch solvent out of the barrel before firing a shot.

BORE GUIDE      A round tube which keeps the cleaning rod straight during the cleaning stroke, and keeps solvent from dripping into the trigger and the bedding.

BUG HOLE      Benchrest slang for a tiny group. Not necessarily a finished group. "I had my first four into a bug hole."

BUG TURBULENCE      1. Slang-excuse for why a shot didn't impact where it was supposed to, caused by the beating of a bugs wings. "That bullet was deflected by bug turbulence."
2. Being deceived by a bug which landed on your target, thinking it was the last shot and holding off to fill in the "group". A definite bummer when the supposed "shot" flies away!

BULL BARREL      A term for heavier than standard barrels made for target use. Heavier barrels dissipate heat better, and are usually more accurate than lighter barrels.

BURNING RATE      The relative quickness at which a type of powder burns. A rough approximation of "faster" or "slower".

BUSHING      A steel disk, or tube, with an accurately sized hole used in the neck sizing die, when the case neck is forced into the hole it reduces the neck dimensions. Sized in increments of .001″ interchangeable bushings give any desired neck tension.

BUTTON      Term for a carbide tool which presses the lands and grooves into a barrel when pulled through the barrel during "button rifling".

# C

**CALLING THE SHOT**   Fixing in you mind the sight picture just as the shot went off. The shooter should know where the shot landed before looking back at the target.

**CANT**   Any deviation in a guns vertical axis from the true vertical. With correct sight alignment cant to the left or right will change the position of bullet impact.

**CASE**   The brass which holds the bullet, powder, and primer.

**CASE TRIMMING**   Removing metal from the open end of the case to get all the cases to the same length, and below maximum allowable length.

**CASH OPTION**   At many events there is an informal gathering of money, to be redistributed after each match to the shooter of the smallest group.

**CHASE**   To readjust aim on subsequent shots because the first didn't land where expected. "Had to chase the first shot, it was two rings high."

**CHICKEN CHOKER**   A group of Pennsylvania natives who make up the most successful four man team in benchrest competition. A core group of six qualifies to represent the group in the major matches.

**CLICK(S)**   Benchrest slang for the unit of measure on the re-worked, ratcheting, powder measures, "I went up a click on the powder measure".

**CONDITION**   Benchrest term for the weather during the firing of a shot. A combination of the wind, light, and mirage. "That condition is worth a bullet and a half to the left".

**CONE FACE BOLT**   A bolt where the nose is cut on an angle. A matching angle is cut into the rear of the barrel, it makes cartridge feeding quicker and easier.

**COPPER FOULING**   When bullets pass through the barrel they deposit small amounts of jacket material on the bore. It's detrimental to accuracy.

**CREEP**   1. Reference to trigger pull. Movement between full finger pressure and sear release. See SLACK.
2. What you think of the shooter at the Super Shoot who just beat your .073" group with a .072"

**CROWN**   Careful chamfering done on the end of the barrel making sure it's square to the bore to ensure the bullets delivery into flight the same on each shot.

C.U.P.  Copper Units of Pressure The modern term used in the measurement of pressure developed during the firing of a shot. Taken in a special pressure gun, the amount a copper cylinder gets crushed is measured and compared to a table.

## D

DAISY  Used to indicate wind direction, and velocity. A plastic pin wheel adapted from the common garden decoration.

DE-CAPPER  A pin, either in a tool or hand held, which is used to remove fired primers from the case

DIRT HURTER  Slang for a group which all it did was hurt the dirt in the backstop. A poor effort, when you needed a "slack grabber".

DOPING  Determining by previous shots, sighters, or wind flags, sometimes by dead reckoning, where to hold the next shot so it will impact the group. "I doped the condition and dropped the shot right in the middle of the group."

DOUBLE  1. When side-by-side shooters fire at exactly the same time, and a noise flinch, or concussion effect causes one of the shots to be a flyer. "I doubled with the guy next to me."
2. When a shot lands in the exact hole of a previous shot. "I doubled the first hole."

DRIFT ASSEMBLY  The top and stem from a hand held bullet seater.

DUMMY CARTRIDGE  A cartridge made without primer or powder, used to check seating depth of the bullet.

## E

EROSION  The by-product of a lot of shots through a barrel. The heat from the shots gives the first section of the barrel an "alligator hide" look. When pieces of the alligator hide flake off accuracy is substantially reduced.

EXCITEMENT  What happens to your heart when the first four shots go into a "bug-hole".

## F

FELL OFF THE BENCH  Slang for ruining a group on the last shot. "I had a .150″ till I fell off the bench."

FIRE FORMING  Expanding a case to a different, or larger size by firing it in the new chamber.

FIRING PIN PROTRUSION    The amount a firing pin sticks out beyond the bolt face at the instant of maximum forward travel.

FLAT BASE    The style of bullet without a taper on its rear end

FLUTING    Machining longitudinal grooves in a barrel, or bolt. Used to remove weight, and increase surface area for maximum cooling. Not recommended for big bruisers like the .30-378 Weatherby wildcat.

FLY BUSTER    An extremely accurate rifle. So accurate it can hit flies at 100 yards. In the past there were matches where competitors shot at flies printed on a target.

FLYER    A shot which lands where it's not expected. "It threw a flyer two rings away from the group."

FOULED    A rifle which has burned powder and copper residue built up in its bore, shots no longer go where expected. "It's fouled."

FOULING    The compound left in the bore after one or more shots.

FOULING SHOT    Often called a "fouler", a shot fired after cleaning, used to leave fouling in the barrel such as would be left by each shot fired for score, in some rifles fouling shots have a different point of impact.

FPS    Feet Per Second. The distance a bullet travels in one second. With the advent of the lightweight, reasonably priced, chronograph its a useful accuracy tool.

FREE FLOATING    To have the barrel touch no more than the first inch of the stock in front of the action. Most solid bottom actions have no barrel/stock contact. "It has a free floating barrel."

FREE RECOIL    Shooting a light recoiling rifle, without holding it, while it rests solely on the sandbags. The only shooter contact is at the trigger, the aim is changed by adjusting the sandbags.

## G

GARBAGE    Benchrest slang for how a group turned out, or the state of the equipment.

GLUE-IN    Attaching the barreled action solidly to the stock by epoxying the two together at the action.

GRAND AGGREGATE    The average of a 100 and 200 yard aggregate yields a Grand Aggregate (100 + 200 divided by 2). If your 100 yard aggregate was .2822 and the 200 yard aggregate was .3458 the Grand Aggregate would be .3140.

GROOVE

1. The indentation cut, or pressed into a rifle barrel which combined with the lands forms the rifling. Groove diameter is the distance between the bottoms of opposing grooves. In a 6mm Hart Stainless steel match barrel this would be .2430″

2. Slang for consistent shooting. "I'm in a groove."

# H

H322

A fast burning rifle powder made by the Hodgdon company which a large portion of the benchrest community uses in their small benchrest cartridges.

HEADSPACE

The distance between the bolt face and the surface which arrests case movement in the chamber. Excessive headspace can be dangerous.

HANDLOADING

The process of reloading ammunition with precise hand tools. Usually done to improve accuracy.

HEAVY BENCH

The type of rifle for which there are no size, weight, or configuration restrictions.

HEAVY VARMINT

The most popular class in benchrest. Weight limit is 13 1/2 pounds, any caliber is allowable.

HOLD or HOLD-OVER

Same as windage, changing the position of the crosshairs based upon conditions. "I held the last shot into the condition a bullet and a half and got a good group."

HOLLOW POINT

The only style bullet used in benchrest, with a cavity at its tip, the bulk of the lead core is close to the center of gravity. It helps stabilize the bullet, tests prove it to be the most accurate style of bullet.

I-BEAM

Machined I-Beams are used as the plate on which most return to battery rifles are built. Also used in some of the lighter weight classes to provide rigidity without excess weight.

IBS

International Benchrest Shooters - The organization which runs benchrest events in the Northeast and Internationally.

IRON MONSTER

A return-to-battery rifle

# J

JAG

The removable tip for a cleaning rod which is used to push a cleaning patch through the barrel.

## K

**KEYHOLE** A bullet which fails to stabilize, and passes through the target partially sideways rather than point on.

**KNOCKOUT PIN** The pin in a neck sizing die which removes the fired primer during the resizing operation.

## L

**LAND** The raised rib standing between the grooves in a rifle barrel.

**LAP** Some match grade barrels receive their final finish with a "lap". A soft metal slug is coated with mild abrasive and stroked through the barrel to remove minor tooling marks and high spots.

**LEADE** The throat portion of a chamber. It's the beginning of the rifling in the barrel. The lands have been slightly cut away to ease the engagement of the bullet.

**LET-UP** A decrease in wind velocity. "Don't shoot in the blow, wait for a let-up."

**LIGHT VARMINT** One of the 10 1/2 pound classes where any caliber is allowable.

**LOADING DENSITY** The percentage of the case which is filled with powder with the bullet in place. In benchrest we try to achieve 100%, that is, leaving no air space between the powder and the bullet.

**LOCK TIME** The time, measured in milliseconds, it takes for the firing pin to strike the primer after being released by the sear. One of the reasons the Model 70 fell out of favor in benchrest.

**LOT NUMBER** Different bulk production is assigned a specific number. Used in benchrest when an accurate component is found, quantity purchase of the exact lot number ensures consistent results.

## M

**MACHINE REST** Also called an UNLIMITED REST, or RETURN-TO-BATTERY rest, a device which supports and guides the rifle during the shot. Used to completely eliminate human holding error.

**MAKE WEIGHT** At every benchrest match rifles are weighed to ensure they aren't over the allowable limit. You have to "make weight".

MATCH      Used interchangeably for either an individual group or the entire event. "I just shot the first record match", or "I'm at my third match this year".

MINUTE OF ANGLE (MOA)      An angular measurement used to describe the accuracy of a rifle. It's 1/60th of a degree, or 1.047 inches at 100 yards, generally acknowledged as one inch at 100 yards, two inches at 200 yards, and three inches at 300 yards.

MIRAGE      The bending of light waves caused by different densities of air, humidity, and their movement.

MIRAGE BOARD      A printed piece of paper with alternating black and white horizontal stripes used to read the mirage.

MOVING BACKER      A piece of cardboard, or paper, which is pulled horizontally behind the target as a group is fired, it ensures the proper number of shots is in a bug hole.

## N

NBRSA      The organization which runs benchrest events throughout the country other than the Northeast.

NECK SIZING      The style of partial resizing benchrest shooters use to get the best accuracy. The brass case body is not resized, since it has expanded to fit the individual chamber it's left alone. Only the neck is reduced, just enough to hold a new bullet.

NECK TENSION      The amount of "grip" a case neck has on a bullet.

## O

OAL      Over-All-Length. The final length of a loaded round.

OFFICIAL SCREAMER      A patch is given by PRECISION SHOOTING Magazine to recognize tiny groups. For five shot groups below .100" @ 100 yards, below .200" @ 200 yards, .399" @ 300 yards. 10 shot screamers can be a bit larger. "I shot an Official Screamer."

OGIVE      Pronounced o-jive, the pointed forward portion of a bullet, all the bullet forward of the bearing surface.

OH-MY-GOSH      One of the frequently heard expressions on days when the wind is switching quickly, interchangeable with S.O.B.

## P

PATCH      To run small pieces of cloth through the bore to remove cleaning solvent. "I'll go to the line after patching my rifle."

PARALLAX        The mismatch of the picture formed by the objective lens not being on the same plane as the cross hairs. It can be observed by slowly moving the eye side-to-side in the field of view. If the cross-hairs move on the target, there's parallax.

PAPER PUNCHER     Term for a target rifle or shooter.

PATTERN        Benchrest slang for a poor group, used in reference to a shotgun pattern. Expressed with irony. "I shot a big pattern on that one."

PEDESTAL        The adjustable front rest which supports the rifle.

PILLAR BED        A style of bedding for bolt in rifles which lessens the chance of impact shift caused by moisture or heat changes.

PIN WHEEL        1. A shot that lands in the exact center of the bulls eye. 2. Rotating wheel used to show wind direction and velocity.

PORT        Opening in the left or right side of the receiver for placing the cartridge into the action.

POWDER MEASURE     An adjustable device which gives repeatable volumetric charges of gunpowder every time the handle is worked. A benchrester using a high quality measure can throw charges within + or - .1 grain.

PPC        The Pindell-Palmisano Cartridge, which, in one form or another, is used by 90% of the current benchresters.

## Q

QUIT        Something you'll never do once you get hooked on benchrest shooting.

## R

RAIN SHOT        During a rain storm if a rain drop gets into the muzzle it causes the bullet to deflect significantly.

RANGE AGGREGATE     See Aggregate.

READ        The ability to notice conditions and hold the shot appropriately to get it to impact in the group. "I read the conditions right, held off a bullet hole and put it into the group."

RECHAMBER        When accuracy falls off, cutting off the old portion of the rifle barrel, and reaming in a new chamber. To remove the section with damaged lands and improve accuracy by moving up to a fresher portion of the barrel

RECORD MATCH     A match which counts towards the aggregate score.

RECORD SHOT    An individual bullet fired at the top portion of the target, which will be counted in the group size. There are five record shots in the varmint classes, ten record shots in Heavy Bench.

RECORD TARGET    1. The top portion of the benchrest target on which must be fired five shots in Heavy Varmint and Light Varmint, or ten shots in Heavy Bench.
2. Shooting a group which is better than any shot before.

RELAY    The people filling the benches who shoot first comprise the first relay. The next group to shoot would be the second relay, etc. At a big match with hundreds of shooters there might be five or six relays of shooters.

RESTS    The pedestal and sandbags, or machine device off which rifles are shot.

RELOAD    Using carefully matched cases over again by replacing primer, powder and bullet. Benchresters have used one brass case for as many as 1000 firings.

RETURN-TO-BATTERY    Some Heavy Bench rifles use rests which allow them to come into position and be fired without resighting.

REVERSE    The change of wind or mirage from one direction to the other. "I lost the last shot in a reverse, it dropped out half an inch."

## S

SANDBAGS    In the early days these were cloth bags filled with sand. They've evolved into high quality leather bags, made in several sizes, and styles, which support the front and rear of the rifle.

SCOPE    The high powered, internally adjusted, sighting device placed on top of all benchrest rifles.

SEAR    The part which holds the firing pin while cocked, it's released by the movement of the trigger, allowing the pin to fall.

SEGREGATION    To carefully match brass as to weight and measurement. "These are my segregated match cases."

SHELL HOLDER BOLTFACE    An action without a port. The loaded round is placed in a U shaped shell holder machined into the nose of the bolt, inserted from the rear of the receiver, and locked down for firing. The bolt must be completely withdrawn on every shot. A very accurate design, but much too slow for competitive shooting.

SHOOT or SHOOTER    Used in reference to a very accurate rifle: "It's a shooter", or "it shoots".

SHOULDER MIRAGE    Slang for throwing a shot out of the group with too much shoulder pressure. "What caused that last shot?" "Shoulder mirage."

SIGHTER    1. The bottom portion of a benchrest target on which all fouling and practice shots are taken.
2. Taking a shot at the bottom portion to check how a particular condition moves the bullet.

SIGHTER SUCKERED    Slang for holding a shot based on what a sighter shot indicates, then having the shot land where it's not expected. "I got sighter suckered and the shot landed half an inch away."

SINGLE SHOT    The style of action used in benchrest. With a solid bottom (no magazine) the action is stiffer, supplies more bedding surface and contributes to better accuracy.

SISSY BAG    A sandbag placed between the butt stock and your shoulder on heavy recoiling rifles.

SLACK    Trigger movement before full contact on the sear. Two oz. triggers are adjusted for no slack. See Creep.

SLACK GRABBER    Slang for a great group. "I need a slack grabber to catch the leaders."

SLEEVE    An aluminum or steel cylinder which is epoxied over a round action to increase stiffness and increase bedding surface for glue-ins.

SLING    Slang for where your rear end is after shooting in a full reverse.

SPORTER    One of the 10 1/2 pound classes where the rifle must be .243 bore diameter or larger. Originally developed to promote experimentation.

STATIONARY BACKER    A fixed piece of paper behind every target to reveal cross-fires.

STEERING    Influencing the aim by applying pressure with the hand, shoulder, or cheek.

STOCK    The portion into which is inlet the barreled action. Usually made of fibreglass, or Kevlar.

STOOL SHOOTIN    What we do in benchrest.

SWAGE    The process used by custom bullet makers to assemble their accurate little jewels. A die of the final size accepts the jacket and core, great pressure is exerted to expand the bullet to final dimension, and bond the two together.

SWITCH    The same as a reverse. Wind or mirage changing over from one direction to the other.

SWITCH BARREL    A rifle with multiple barrels. Usually one designed to change from Light Varmint to Heavy Varmint by putting on a longer, heavier, barrel and sometimes more weight in the buttstock.

## T

TACK DRIVER    An extremely accurate rifle. "This baby's a tack driver."

TIME LIMIT    How long you're allowed, to shoot a group in a match. In the Varmint classes it's seven minutes for five record shots. In Heavy Bench it's 12 minutes for ten record shots. An unlimited number of sighter shots may be fired during this time.

TONG TOOL    A nutcracker type reloading tool which is reworked to provide precise neck sizing.

TRUE    To clean up an action by getting all right angles square. A definite accuracy enhancer.

TWIST    The length of bore the bullet must pass through to rotate 360 degrees, expressed in inches. For the 6PPC the twist rate is one turn in 14″ for 68 grain bullets.

TWO GUN, THREE GUN, FOUR GUN    The combination of the Grand Aggregates from all the classes shot during a match. The hardest to win, and the most valuable trophy.

TWO OUNCE TRIGGER    A precise match trigger, usually without safety which can be set to release at as low as two ounces.

## U

UPSET    1. Under high pressure all metals are slightly elastic, when a shot is fired the base of the bullet deforms slightly to fill the shape of the barrel. It helps seal the expanding gasses.
2. How we get after spoiling a "bug hole."

## V

VARMINT    Creatures like woodchucks, prairie dogs, and coyote's which started benchrest's founders on their search for extreme accuracy. The word is picked up and used in the name of the two most popular classes, Heavy Varmint, and Light Varmint.

## W

WAILING WALL     The area where targets are placed after being scored. In NBRSA competition the targets must be left throughout the entire match. "There's some lousy groups on the wailing wall."

WARM-UP     The first match of a range aggregate, fired before the first record match.

WEATHER REPORT     Term for a lousy target which shows all the deflection possible from the conditions. Usually means the shooter got caught by a gust or reverse.

WILDCAT     A non standard cartridge for which there is no factory loaded ammunition. Usually designed by an individual looking for "something better."

WIND FLAG     An indicator designed to give the shooter quantifiable information on the movement of the wind.

WINDAGE     In a lateral wind the amount the sights are moved into the condition to allow a shot to impact the group.

WIND DRIFT     How far a breeze pushes the bullet before it impacts with the target.

WITNESS MARKS     Small punch marks on the side of the barrel and action. When the barrel is screwed into the receiver and the marks are aligned they ensure correct headspace and barrel tightness.

## X-Y-Z

*The authors battle scarred CPS Light Varmint proves there's more than one way to skin a cat.*

# APPENDIX A

# Suppliers & Gunsmiths

When you send these guys a letter requesting a catalog remember to send a couple bucks to cover postage and handling.
**KEY** M = Manufacturer.    G = Gunsmith.    S = Supplier of benchrest equipment.

Audy Adams
Rt 5, Box 175
Tyler, TX 75706
(214) 882-4597

Harold R. Broughton    MG
RT #1
Big Spring, TX 79720

Bruno Shooters Supply    S
10 - 5th St.
Kelayres, PA 18231
(717) 929-1791

Dietz Gun Shot    GS
Rt. 7, Box 189
New Braunfels, TX 78130

Douglas Barrels, Inc.    MG
5504 Big Tyler Road
Charleston, WV 25313-1398

Geo. M. Fullmer    G
2499 Mavis St.
Oakland, CA 94601

David Gentry    G
314 N. Hoffman
Belgrade, MT 59714

Jim Greenawalt    GS
102 Brandon Rd.
Yonkers, NY 10704

Clarence Hammonds    GS
RD #4, Box 504
Red Lion, PA 17356

Hart Rifle Barrels, Inc.    MGS
RD No. 2
LaFayette, NY 13084
(315) 677-9841

Robert W. Hart & Son,
Inc.    MGS
401 Montgomery Street
Nescopeck, PA 18635
(717) 752-3655

Ron Hoehn   G
1430 East Duchesne
Florissant, MS 63031

Dale Hutcherson   G
1406 Wichita ST.
Pasadena, TX 77502

Jarrett Rifles   GS
Route # 1, Box 411
Jackson, SC 29831

Kelbly, Inc.   MGS
7222 Dalton Fox Lake Road
No. Lawrence, OH 44666
(216) 683-4674

Lilja Precision, Inc.   MG
245 Compass Creek Road
PO Box 372
Plains, MT 59859

Seely Masker   GS
261 Washington Ave.
Pleasantville, NY 10570

Glenn Newick   S
6601 Kirby Drive #527
Houston, TX 77005

Bob Pease Accuracy   S
PO Box 310787
New Braunfels, TX 78131-0787
(512) 625-1342

Permian Shooters' Supply   S
PO Box 60421
Midland, TX 79711
(915) 563-4341 or 800-351-1466

Sinclair International, Inc.   MGS
718 Broadway
New Haven, IN 46774
(219) 493-1858

Shilen Rifles, Inc.   MGS
205 Metro Park Blvd.
Ennis, TX 75119
(214) 875-5318

Clay Spencer   GS
Route #1, Box 546
Scottsville, VA 24590
(804) 293-4922

Robert A. White   GS
8 New Jersey Ave
Hopatcong, NJ 07849
(201) 663-5159

Wiseman/McMillan Barrels   MG
PO Box 3427
Bryan, TX 77805

Custom Action Makers

Hall Mfg.
1801 Yellow Leaf Rd.
Clanton, AL 35045
(205) 755-4094

Robert W. Hart & Son, Inc.
401 Montgomery Street
Nescopeck, PA 18635
(717) 752-3655

Kelbly, Inc.
(Stolle actions)
7222 Dalton Fox Lake Road
No. Lawrence, OH 44666
(216) 683-4674

MCS Inc.
34 Delmar Drive
Brookfield, CT 06804
(203) 775-1013

Wichita Arms, Inc.
PO box 11371
Wichita, KS 67211

Rifle Barrel Makers

Harold R. Broughton
RT #1, Box 447
Big Spring, TX 79720

Douglas Barrels, Inc.   MG
5504 Big Tyler Road
Charleston, WV 25313-1398

H-S Precision, Inc.
PO Box 512
Prescott, AZ 86301

Hart Rifle Barrels, Inc.
RD No. 2
LaFayette, NY 13084
(315) 677-9841

Krieger Barrels
N114 W. 18697 Clinton Dr.
Germantown, WI 53022

Lilja Precision, Inc.
245 Compass Creek Road
PO Box 372
Plains, MT 59859

Pence Precision Barrels
RR #2, Rd. 900 S.
S. Whitley, IN 46787

Rocky Mountain Rifle Works, Ltd.
(Mark Chanlynn)
1707 14th St.
Boulder, CO 80302
(303) 443-9189

Schneider Rifle Barrels, Inc.
12202 N. 62 Pl.
Scottsdale, AZ 85254

Shilen Rifles, Inc.
205 Metro Park Blvd.
Ennis, TX 75119
(214) 875-5318

Wiseman/McMillan Barrels
PO Box 3427
Bryan, TX 77805

Bullet Makers There are dozens of benchrest bullet makers; those listed have high enough production to sell large quantities each year.

Berger Bullets
Walt Berger
4234 N. 63rd Ave.
Phoenix, AZ 85033
(602) 846-5791

Bruno Bullets
Lester Bruno
10 - 5th St.
Kelayres, PA 18231
(717) 929-1791

Fowlers
Jef Fowler
3731 McKelvey St.
Charlotte, NC 28215
(704) 568-7661

Rubright Bullets
Brian Rubright
1008 S. Quince Rd
Walnutport, PA 18088
(215) 767-1339

S.G. Bullets
Speedy Gonzalez
PO Box 108
1191-A South Loop
Stephenville, TX 76401

Tools and Supplies

Armor Metal Products
(Portable shooting benches)
PO Box 4609
Helena, MT 59604

B-Square Co.
(Tools, barrel vises, rests,
arbor presses. Lots of goodies)

Bald Eagle Precision Machine Co.
(Front rests and arbor presses)
101 Allison Street
Lock Haven, PA 17745

Custom Products - Neil Jones
(Benchrest tools of all sorts)
RD 1, Box 483A
Saegertown, PA 16433

Davidson Products for Shooters
(Aluminum sleeves, action
wrenches, and bullet pullers)
2020 Huntington Dr.
Las Cruces, NM 88001

Forster Products
(Benchrest tools)
87 Lanark Ave.
Lanark, IL 61046

Hanned Precision
(Cast bullet tool)
PO Box 2888
Sacramento, CA 95812

Henriksen Tool Company
(Chamber reamers, gauges)
PO Box 668
Phoenix, OR 97535

Tony Hidalgo
(Adjustable shooting stools)
12701 SW 9th Place
Davie, FL 33325

JGS Precision Tool Mfg.
(Chamber reamers)
1141 So. Sumner Rd.
Coos Bay, OR 97420

Marquart Precision Company
(Neck turners)
Box 1740
Prescott, AZ 86302

MTM Molded Products Company
(Ammo boxes)
PO Box 14117
Dayton, OH 45414

Optical Services Co.
(Scope work)
10236 Woodway
El Paso, TX 79925

Premier Reticles
(Scope work)
Route 3, Box 369
Wardensville, VW 26851

Protektor Model
(Sandbags)
7 Ash St.
Galeton, PA 16922

Redding-Hunter, Inc.
(Reloading supplies)
1089 Starr Road
Cortland, NY 13045

RIT/NRA Summer
Gunsmithing Schools
College of Fine & Applied Arts
PO Box 9887
Rochester, NY 14623-0887

Rorschach Precision Products
(Bullet making dies)
PO Box 151613
Irving, TX 75015

Venco Industries, Inc.
(Shooters Choice products)
16770 Hill Top Park Pl.
Chagrin Falls, OH 44022

White Rock Tool & Die
(They rent chamber reamers;
it holds down costs on one
shot chamber jobs)
6400 North Brighton Avenue
Kansas City, Missouri 64119

Whitetail Design & Engineering
(Primer pocket uniformers)
9421 E. Mannsiding Road
Clare, MI 48617

Wilke Machinery Company
(Machinery and tools)
120 Derry Court
York, PA 17402

Check if there are any benchrest
clubs in your area. In most cases the
listed address is for the benchrest
contact. Send a self addressed
stamped envelope for information
about the club nearest you.

IBS BENCHREST CLUBS

Camillus Sportsmen's Club
Hank Gonnella
420 Hawley Ave.
Camillus, NY 13203

Capitol City R & P
Joe Gilbert
17 Forest Ave.
Augusta, ME 04330

Central Jersey R&P Club
Geza Nagy
436 S. 5th Ave
Highland Park, NJ 08904

Dunhams Bay Fish & Game Club
Walt Hodges
112 Feeder St.
Hudson Falls, NY 12839

Englishtown Benchrest Shooters
Bob White
8 New Jersey Ave
Hopatcong, NJ 07849

Factoryville Sportsmen Club
Paul Ryan
RD1 1005, Pheasant Rd.
Clarks Summit, PA 18411

Fairchance Gun Club
Roy Leckemby
RD2, Box 21
Smithfield, PA 15478

Guthsville Rod & Gun Club
David Kern
PO Box 156
Orefield, PA 18069

I.W.L.A. - York
Charles Kinard
RD4, Box 535
Red Lion, PA 17356

Jefferson County I.W.L.A.
Bob Broyles
905 Red Bud Drive
Forest Hills Estates
Martinsburg, WV 25401

John Palmisano Memorial Range
(Council Cup, PA)
Dr. Lou Palmisano
431 Conklin Town Road
Ringwood, NJ 07456

Mainville Sportsmen Club
Randy Fritz
RD3, Box 572
Bloomsburg, PA 17815

Marksman Gun Club
PO Box 655
Perry, OH 44081

Original 1000 Yard Benchrest Club
Sarah Morgan
PO Box 1413
Williamsport, PA 17701

Painted Post Field And Stream
Craig Baravelle
PO Box 325
Corning, NY 14830

Pine Tree Rifle Club Inc.
Charles Clark
PO Box 45
Johnstown, NY 12095

Prairie Dog Target Club
Don Deckert
Porcupine, SD 57772

Salisbury Rod & Gun Club
Ron Poisker
100 Lloyd St.
Salisbury, MD 21801

Snow Shoe Gun Club
PO Box 125
Kenai, AK 99611

South Creek Rod & Gun
Jack Deming
RD1 Lawrenceville, PA 16929

Sulphyr Springs R&G
John Pfleegor
304 South Market St.
Muncy, PA 17756

Thurmont Conservation Club
Richard Pryor
11113 Putnam Road
Thurmintk MD 21788

Titusville Sportsmen's Club
Larry Sheats
Box 110
Titusville PA 16354

Union County Sportsmen
Richard Altemus
RD1
Millmont, PA 17845

## INTERNATIONAL IBS CLUBS

A.F.T.B.R.
Jean Claude Braconi
14 Rue Des Soleil
Nice, 06100
France

Benchrest Shooters of Canada
Wayne Miller
Box 238
Leader, SA S0N 1H0
Canada

DBRV
Peter Hammerich
Sollinge 1
Heiden 4284
West Germany

Penticton Shooting Sports
Ron Johnston
Site 35 Comp 3 RR3
Penticton BC V2A 7K8
Canada

Selkirk Benchrest Club
Murray Benson
10 Park Road
Selkirk, MA R1A 0B3
Canada

Sport Shooters Association
of Australia
Brendan Atkinson
418 Glyburn Road
Erindale 5066
Australia

U.T.I.B.R.
Via Tinzonni 4
Bologna 40137
Italy

## NBRSA BENCHREST CLUBS

Eastern Region

Blue Grass Sportsman's League
Joe Jarrell
304 Mocking Bird Lane
Lexington, KY 40503

Chippewa County Shooting As-
siciation
Joseph Haller
Rt 1, Box 117 Nicolet Rd.
Sault Sainte Marie, MI 49783

Chippewa Rifle Club
Nelson Berger
11374 Mt. Eaton Rd
Marshalville, OH 44635

Crumlin Sportsmen's Association
Jim Fedorowich
91 Deveron Cresent
London, ON N5Z 4B6 Canada

Fairchance Gun Club
Roy Leckemby
Rt 2, Box 21
Smithfield, PA 15478

Fairfield Sportsman's
Orlin Gilkerson
4624 River Rd.
Fairfield, OH 45014

Holton Gun and Bow Club
Al Fay
2704 Ducey
Muskegon, MI 49442

Kane Fish and Game Club
Dick Lockwood
Box 112
Kane, PA 16735

Kelbly's Rifle Range
George Kelbly, Sr.
7222 Dalton Fox Lake Rd.
North Lawrence, OH 44666

Mackinac Straits Shooters
Laroy Hill
11 South Boundry Rd.
St. Ignace, MI 49781

McKinley B.R. Shooters
Harvey LeChat
12085 Wooster St. N.W.
Canton, OH 44646

Reed's Run Rifle Club
Leora Demeter
1907 Franklin Place, NW
Canton, OH 44709

Shelby County
Deer Hunters Assoc.
Jim Boetcher
11 Piqua Circle
Enon, OH 45323

Gulf Coast Region

Austin Rifle Club
Frank Wilson
4904 Rollingwood St.
Austin, TX 78746

Baton Rouge & Pistol Club
Jimmie Broussard
11785 Foster Rd.
Baton Rouge, LA 70811

Central Texas Bench Rest
Shooters Inc.
George Belcher
318 Gabe Dr.
Kerrville, TX 78028

Comanche Springs Rifle & Pistol
Club
Charley McIntyre
Box 1413
Fort Stockton, TX 79735

Corpus Christi Rifle & Pistol Club
PO Box 7117
Corpus Christi, TX 78415

Hub City Rifle & Pistol Club
Louis Langlinais
932 Hugh Wallis Rd.
Lafayette, LA 70501

Menard Gun Club
Wayne Davis
Box 352
Menard, TX 76859

Midland Shooters, Inc.
Brad Calhoun
3303 Travis
Midland, TX 79703

Navarro Gun Club
PO Box 488
Corsicana, TX 75110

Orange Gun Club
D.L. Broussard
PO Box 95
Orangefield, TX 77639

Pearland Sportsman Club
PO Box 1127
League City, TX 77573

San Angelo Gun Club
Billy A. Curl
3610 Millbrook Dr.
San Angelo, TX 77904

Seymour Gun Club
Scott Hunter, Jr.
1612 Buchanan St.
Wichita Falls, TX 76309

Southwest Louisiana Rifle & Pistol
Club
James Neal
1203 California St.
Lake Charles, LA 70605

Shooters Supply Co. & Range
James Tschoepe
756 Burges St
Seguin, TX 78155

Tiger Island Gun Club
PO Box 2106
Morgan City, LA 70381

Tomball Gun Club
Mike Scheltz
12701 New Kentucky Rd.
Cypress, TX 77429

Mid-Continent Region

Colorado Bench Rest Shooters, Inc.
Dan Dowling
10919 W. 59th Place
Arvada, CO 80004

Kansas City·Mill Creek Rifle Club
Larry Kuse
8112 W. 89th St.
Overland Park, KS 36212

Okie Shooters
Rex Reneau
7409 N.W. 28 Terr.
Bethany, OK 73008

Sandhill Rifle and Pistol Club
Steve Ochs
3023 17th
Great Bend, KS 67530

Springfield Rifle Club
Mike Bishop
409 South Avenue
Springfield, MO 65806

Tulsa Bench Rest Club
Wayne Blackketter
7811 E. 2nd St
Tulsa, OK 74112

Weld County Fish and
Wildlife Association, Inc.
John Ambler
2025 Cheshire St.
Ft. Collins, CO 80526

Mississippi Valley Region

B&R Gun Club
Bill Gwin
2302 State Rd 38 East
Westfield, IN 46074

Beeson's Rifle Range
Jon Leu
860 Hwy 30 East #10
New Haven, IN 46774

Benchrest Rifle Club of St. Louis
Rich Griffin
54 Dawn Ridge Dr.
Hazelwood, MO 63042

Egyptian Rifle and Pistol Club
Marvin Voss
RR1 Dedr Lane 15
Carbondale, IL 62901

Northeast Region

Camillus Sportsmen's Club
Hank Gonnella
420 Hawley Ave.
Camillus NY 13203

North Central Region

Buffalo Rifle Club
Larry Mosebar
PO box 384
Story, WY 82842

Cedar Rapids Bench Rest Club
Ed Kvarda
2406 Ellis Blvd. NW
Cedar Rapids, IA 52405

Cody Shooting Complex
Huck Hutson
Box 999
Red Loge, MT 59068

Council Bluffs Rifle and Pistol Club
Robert Dodd
8230 Wilson Dr.
Ralston, NB 68127

Minnetonka Game and Fish Club
Don Judd
645 20th Ave. NW
New Brighton, MN 55112

Oak Hills Gun Club
Jim Bounds
3802 26 St
Moline, IL 61265

Prairie Dog Target Club
Don Deckert
Porcupine, SD 57772

River City Rifle and Pistol Club
Terry Meyer
RR1 Box 50
Thornton, IA 50479

Wilton Rifle Club
Dennis Shepard
12 Debbe Ave.
Muscatine, IA 52761

Northwest Region

Entiat Benchrest Club
Ted Whitehall
box 5694
Dinkleman Canyon Rd.
Entiat, WA 98222

LaGrande Rifle and Pistol Club
Greg Vergari
Rt. #4, Box 4411
LaGrande, OR 97850

Namaka Bench Rest Shooters Club
Al Mirdoch
Box 3070 Station B
Calgary, Alberta T2M 4L6
Canada

Prickly Pear Shortsmen's Assoc.
Lee Andrews
401 S. California St
Helena, MT 59604

Puget Sound Bench Rest Club
Jim Folwell
1419 Sweetwaterloop SW
Olympia, WA 98502

Snow Shoe Gun Club
Steve Meyer
PO Box 125
Kenai, AK 99611

Tri-County Gun Club
Larry Schwantes
5160 SW Custer St.
Portland OR 97219

Western Montana Fish and Game
Association
Bill Cote
3314 Paxson
Missoula, MT 59801

Southeastern Region

Alleghany County Rifle Assoc.
Charles Joines
Box 306
Sparta, NC 28675

Brunswick Gun Club
John King
111 Brook Ave
South Hill, VA 23970

Buccaneer Gun Club
Don Sloop
3306 Bragg Dr
Wilmington, NC 28403

Central Florida Bench Rest Club
James Hare
5700 Palm Dr.
Ft Pierce, FL 33702

Fayette County Gun Club
Charles Lahay
131-14th Ct NW
Fayette, AL 35555

Gallatin Gun Club
Murray Anderson
1109 57th Ave. N
Nashville, TN 37209

Greenville Gun Club
Skip Peden
Route #8, Box 187
Piedmont, SC 29673

Izaak Walton Bench Rest Club
Rt. 5, 300 Manakin Rd.
Midlothian, VA 23113

Kettlefoot Rod & Gun Club
Claude Smith
96 Cox Rd
Bristol, TN 24201

Long Creek Rifle & Pistol Club
Larry Earp
1029 Byrum St.
Charlotte, NC 28216

Memphis R & R Association Inc.
George M. Busby
3887 St. Elmo
Memphis, TN 38128

Mid-Carolina Rifle Club
Jerry Shelton
217 Cedar Vale Rd
Lexington, SC 29072

River Bend Gun Club
Joe Carlisle
31 Gwinnet Dr. Apt 5
Lawrenceville, GA 30245

Roanoke R & R Club
Ted Manning
RD4, Box 416B
Salem, VA 24153

Rowan County Wildlife Assoc.
Don Sutton
(704) 933-2885

Twin City R & P Club
236 Old Farm Rd
Roanoke Rapids, NC 27870

Volunteer Rifle & Pistol Club
Doug Hubbard
6705 Pine Grove Rd
Knoxville, TN 37914

Watauga Gun Club
Larry Isenhour
Rt 1, Box 284A
Zionville, NC 28698

Wyoming Antelope Club
John Jessip
10900 Roosevelt Blvd. No.
St. Petersburg, FL 33702

Southwest Region

Ben Avery Bench Rest Range
Walt Berger
4234 N. 63rd Ave
Phoenix, AZ 85033

California Bench Rest
Shooters Association
Dennis Thornbury
1114 S. McAuliff Rd
Visalia, CA 93277

Carson Rifle and Pistol Club
Dick Cundiff
2549 Sneddon Way
Carson City, NV 89701

Desert Sportsman's Rifle
and Pistol Club
G.R. Shutt
1985 Duneville
Las Vegas, NV 89102

Southern Utah Bench Rest Assoc.
Rick Adams
24 E. 750 South St.
St. George, Utah 84770

INTERNATIONAL
NBRSA CLUBS

A.F.T.B.R.
Jean Jacques Cristau
13 Rue Des Bluets
78650 Beynes
France

Bench Rest Dolomiti
Toni Negri
Via Alemagna, 1
39034 Dobbiaco (BZ)
Italy

B.B.R.S.A.
Neil Jones
48 Stafford Lane
Hednesford, Staffordshire
England

# The Riflemans Library

The library list starts with the "big" books, those which deal specifically with benchrest, then goes into others with accuracy related information for the interested rifleman.

Whelen, Col. Townsend, THE ULTIMATE IN RIFLE PRECISION Published in 1949, 1950, 1951, 1954, 1958. Infantry Journal Press published the first two editions, then the Telegraph Press, and the Stackpole Company for the last two editions. Col Townsend Whelen edited all five editions, but there were various authors of the individual chapters. The original "handbook" for benchrest. Though much of the information is dated, and some of the books are similar, they're all interesting from a historical perspective. I paid a paltry $10.00 for a 1954 copy from a used book dealer who didn't know what he had, and $75.00 for a first edition through a dealer. No matter what the price they merit it.

Wallack, L.R.(Bob), MODERN ACCURACY, Greenberg, 1951. A 151 page jewel which gives an overview of benchrest history. Hard to find, but worth it.

Page, Warren, THE ACCURATE RIFLE, Winchester Press, 1973, (paperback editions by Stoeger). An important book which gives meaningful insight into benchrest shooting, though the equipment information is dated. A "must read" for any benchrest shooter. Stocked by R.W. Hart & Son, and Bob Pease.

That's it for the benchrest specific books. A grand total of seven. With all the hot air that's thrown around at a match you would think there would have been others who put forth the effort to create a book. There are many additional sources of information which the interested rifleman should look up.

Ackley, Parker O., HANDBOOK FOR SHOOTERS AND RELOADERS, Publishers Press, 1962.

Ackley, Parker O., SUPPLEMENT TO THE HANDBOOK FOR SHOOTERS AND RELOADERS, published by author. These two volumes are invaluable for reference material on wildcats.

Anderson, Gary, L., MARKSMANSHIP, International Shooter Development Fund, 1972. A basic instructional booklet which contains the fundamentals of championship level shooting.

Carmichel, Jim, THE MODERN RIFLE, Stoeger Publishing Company, 1975. A good reading book with brief mention of benchrest. Carmichel, Jim, JIM CARMICHEL'S BOOK OF THE RIFLE, Outdoor Life Book, 1985. An excellent book with chapters on benchrest and target rifles.

Crossman, Edward C., SMALL BORE RIFLE SHOOTING, Small Arms Technical Publishing Co., 1927. Interesting historical perspective on shooting rimfires. Also explains that women can whip the men any old day.

Donaldson, Harvey, YOURS TRULY, HARVEY DONALDSON, Wolfe Publishing, 1980. The forty columns Harvey authored for "Handloader" Magazine from 1966 to 1972 with lots of background correspondence.

Greener, W.W., THE GUN AND ITS DEVELOPMENT, first published in 1881, the ninth edition, from 1910, has been reprinted several times by Bonanza. A interesting book which runs down the history of firearms.
Greener, W.W., SHARPSHOOTING FOR SPORT & WAR, Truslove, Hanson & Comba, 1900. "Rifle-shooting is to-day the subject of supreme importance to every Briton, for only by general proficiency in the use of the best weapon can the Empire be maintained, and the national safety secured."

Hatcher, Julian S., HATCHER'S NOTEBOOK, Stackpole, several editions. The standard reference work that might save some time exploring something which was proven useless years ago.

Hudson, W. G., MODERN RIFLE SHOOTING FROM THE AMERICAN STANDPOINT, Laflin & Rand Powder Company, 1903. This book shows how far we've come: "I look upon the 200 yard Shuetzen to survive no matter how popular other branches become."

Kelver, Gerald, RESPECTFULLY YOURS, H.M. POPE, Kelver. Gerald has privately printed several single shot books, support his efforts by buying one of them.

Landis, C.S., TWENTY-TWO CALIBER VARMINT RIFLES, Small Arms Technical Publishing Company, 1947. A real gem filled with wondrous names like the K-Hornet, the .22/4000 Sedgley- Schnerring, the Marciante Blue Streak and others. A "must have" for any serious experimenter.
Landis, C.S., WOODCHUCKS AND WOODCHUCK RIFLES, Greenberg, 1951. Early information on benchrest and single shots. Landis, C.S., .22 CALIBER RIFLE SHOOTING, Small Arms Technical Publishing, 1932. An earlier piece on rimfires.

SPEER RELOADING MANUAL FOR WILDCAT CARTRIDGES, No. 4., Speer Products, 1960. Wildcat information.

Mann, Dr. Franklin W., THE BULLET'S FLIGHT, various publishers, currently Wolfe Publishing. Originally published in 1909 by a scientific experimenter this book completely explores bullet flight.

Ness, F.C., PRACTICAL DOPE ON THE BIG BORES, Stackpole Company, first edition 1948, second edition 1953. Covers the standard cartridges and several wildcats.
Ness, F.C., PRACTICAL DOPE ON THE .22, Military Service Publishing Company, 1947. Covers the .22 centerfires, both standard and wildcat.

Otteson, Stuart, BENCHREST ACTIONS AND TRIGGERS, Wolfe Publishing. Another "must have" that passes along lots of information.
Otteson, Stuart, THE BOLT ACTION, Winchester Press, 1976, and THE BOLT ACTION, VOLUME II, Wolfe Publishing.

Pease, Bob, BOB PEASE COLLECTION, VOLUMES I, II, III. Rambling, spiral bound, collection with lots of benchrest notes and information. Available direct from Bob.

Roberts, Ned, THE MUZZLE LOADING CAP LOCK RIFLE, Roberts, (later reprinted in 1950 by Bonanza). The definitive work on the target muzzle loader.
Roberts, Ned and Waters, Ken, THE BREECH-LOADING SINGLE SHOT MATCH RIFLE, Van Nostrand, 1967 (recently reprinted by Wolfe) The reprint has been updated. A "must have" for the single- shot enthusiast.

Sawyer, Charles W., OUR RIFLES, Cornhill Company, 1920, and Williams Book Store, 1946. Includes rough photographs and notes on some early muzzle loading target rifles.

Sharpe, Phillip B, COMPLETE GUIDE TO HANDLOADING, Funk & Wagnalls Company, 1937 & 1941, now from Wolfe. After reading these 600 pages and seeing what the shooters of the 1930's had to put up with you'll never again complain about copper fouling in your new barrel.

Simmons, Richard F., WILDCAT CARTRIDGES, William Morrow and Company, 1947. Wildcats galore from the days of yore.

Smith, Ray M., THE STORY OF POPE'S BARRELS, Stackpole, 1960. The definitive work on the subject.

Stebbins Henry M. SMALL GAME & VARMINT RIFLES, A.S. Barnes & Company, 1947. Another of the interesting historical perspectives. Note how many of the wildcat books appeared in a three year period.

Wallack, L.R., AMERICAN RIFLE DESIGN AND PERFORMANCE, Winchester Press, 1977. A book with a strong section on benchrest, a pleasant surprise at chapter 19.

Waters, Ken, PET LOADS, Wolfe Publishing. Loading data on over 100 cartridges.

Whelen, Col. Townsend and Angier, Bradford, MISTER RIFLEMAN, Peterson Publishing Company, 1965. Great pictures of Townsends' rifles, includes a chapter on benchrest.

Wooters, John, THE COMPLETE BOOK OF PRACTICAL HAND-LOADING, Stoeger Publishing, 1976. The book which got me started on the right foot. Strong on record keeping, and consistency.

# INDEX